Oil painting of
Unknown Monsignor
By Madge Phillips Abernathy
Circa 1961

Priest

The Last Confession

Royal Phillips

ISBN: 1981314156
ISBN-13: 978-1981314157

DEDICATION

This true story is dedicated
to women who share similar
exploitations.

May we continue
to have the courage
to heal.

CONTENTS

My Story

When I attended a 1962 college writing class with my story, they sent me home saying it could never happen. I refused to stop my pursuit. In 2016, A New York literary agent sent me home and said to write my story as fiction. I refused to stop my pursuit.

In the name of God, Catholic women have been coerced and manipulated by their parish priests to keep silent as they lived in shame with their dark secrets. I refused to stop my pursuit.

I came from a dysfunctional Middle Western background. My mother's strict Catholic upbringing clashed with my father's high degree of Masonic beliefs.

This combination, fueled by their alcoholism set the stage for my rocky survival. In my later teen years after my father's early death, we moved to Palm Springs. My mother consulted an Irish priest to save my soul. Instead, he brought me to damnation.

My aim is to help other women heal as well as their invisible illegitimate sons and daughters.

Now, this finally is my story.

CHAPTER 1

I was home. The nightmare had ended.

The flight from Los Angeles had touched down on the narrow desert runway bordered by tumbleweeds. I descended the passenger ramp into the clear November night and took a long, deep breath.

A middle-aged stocky man with a beaming smile left the group of greeters and headed toward me across the runway. I looked at his Bermuda shorts and tan knobby knees and recognized Father Mike.

"Ah, well," he said in his Irish lilt, "now, you're a sight for sore eyes; a true vision from heaven." He studied me for a moment. "Let me take this for you." He reached for my red plaid cosmetic case and gallantly took my arm.

"Father Mike, what a surprise," I said. "How did you know I'd be on this flight?"

"Your housemaid Greta told me and I wanted to be the first to welcome you home," he said. "Where's your mother?"

"I left her in New Jersey with my brother Merv." I looked at this priest desperate for help. "Father Mike, I need help, can you...? She's been drunk in every country we visited. It was an absolute nightmare. I've never been so embarrassed or humiliated.

1

She made a fool out of herself all over the globe."

"Come now, Royal, it couldn't be that bad."

"Oh, no? What would you say to her wetting her pants on the verandah of the Raffles hotel and the Tim..."

Father Mike stroked my arm, "Calm down, now. You're too lovely to be so upset."

"But I don't know what to do with her and neither does my brother. Where can we get some help for her?"

"Well, the closest AA is in San Bernardino," Father Mike said, struggling to cram my abundant luggage into the trunk of his 1957 Thunderbird, "and here? You're not going to be getting any."

"What about a psychiatrist?"

"There are no psychiatrists in Palm Springs," he said. "Just forget about it."

"What do you mean, forget about it? Are you out of your mind?" I was astounded that he could so dispassionately brush aside my family's biggest problem.

"Soon I'll be back in college and there'll be no one to control her. Don't you have any idea how to help us?" I assumed that a priest would surely have an answer.

But, this priest with the Thunderbird convertible, this priest with two horses, a Western and an English saddle, this priest who was the head of St. Theresa's Parish, which made the most money in the Southern California Diocese, this priest to whom movie stars gave large donations to be padded as tax write-offs, this priest had no advice to give me.

Over the next few days, I unpacked my suitcases, slept, and

swam vigorous laps in the pool. Soon the knot of apprehension that I had grown so used to while traveling with my mother began to loosen.

Father Mike tried to make up for his lack of answers by sweeping me into a whirl of holiday social functions. He had honorary memberships at all four of the best country clubs and invited me to accompany him to the numerous Christmas buffets and dinner dances. He introduced me to his friends who on more than one occasion said jokingly, "Is this another one of your beautiful nieces, Father Mike?"

At the Tennis Club Christmas dance, Father Mike waltzed me all over the floor.

"You're such a wonderful dancer, where did you learn to dance like this, Father?"

"Why, in the seminary in Ireland, Royal, didn't you know they have a special dance class for priests?"

"Oh, yes? Do some of them wear tights and dance ballet?"

"Of course, regular Rudolf Nureyev's."

I relished the freedom to do as I pleased in my mother's absence and after months of being caged with the wicked queen I enjoyed surrendering to the gaiety that this unusual priest provided.

Riding horseback across the cool desert sand one morning, I began to feel safe enough to share my inner feelings.

"Father, I need your help about my boyfriend."

"Of course, Royal, I'd help you with anything. What problems are you having, then?"

"Well, I've been pinned to Doug for two years and Mother

hates him. She hates all my friends. She took me around the world with the hopes that I would forget him."

"And have you?"

"No, the trip made me think of him all the more. But, I don't know if he's lost interest in me while I've been gone."

"Only a fool could lose interest in you."

"Do you really think so? Do you think our love can endure Mother's hate?"

"I think that true love can endure anything. Now don't you be worrying about your mother again"

"But you don't really know her."

"I know I can handle her."

"You mean you will help me with this? Can you talk to her about Doug?"

"Certainly. I'd do anything to help you."

He kicked his dappled grey horse into a gallop. We rode off across the desert.

Sometimes when he took me home at night, after both of us had been drinking too much, he would make what I thought were vaguely romantic overtures. He would brush my cheek with the back of his hand or gently caress my arm as he detailed the plans of our next meeting.

One night after the Racquet Clubs Christmas dance, he kissed me definitely in a non-priestly way. I quickly pulled away.

Father Mike, I have no intentions to tempt you," I said. "You're a priest and I respect that."

I certainly had no designs on this man. I simply enjoyed his company. He was funny, he was Irish and full of tales. He didn't fit my image of a priest. I admired his unconventionality, and I could easily talk to him.

A couple of weeks after I returned to Palm Springs, my brother, Merv, called from New Jersey.

"Royal, Mother has set our guest room on fire and for everyone's safety, I have secured her in a nearby sanitarium. For Christ's sake, M.C. rushed into our bedroom late two nights ago to report that Grandma was having a bonfire in her bedroom."

"Now you understand what I went through dragging her around the world, don't you?" I said sarcastically.

"It must have been a nightmare, Royal."

So, Merv had done what I never had the guts to do. He had committed her.

* * *

Knowing that my mother would definitely be out of the picture for the holidays, I decided to invite Doug to a secret rendezvous. He was home from college for Christmas vacation in Santa Barbara. I could no longer trust Greta since she found all the explicit love letters Doug had written me. He had hoped to seduce me into finally going "all the way" when I returned to college. I had hidden these under the tissue of my shoeboxes and stored them carefully in the back of my closet. Greta had prowled there and promptly revealed them to my mother who in turn made copies of them and attached them to her last will and testament. An ugly scene had occurred.

5

"These will be read by my lawyer, you whore of a daughter, so all will know why I will leave you very little of my estate.", she hissed. Greta's erect German body stood by her side victoriously smug. My heart had been torn apart at this invasion of privacy.

With this in mind, I proposed I meet Doug half-way in Glendale at the home of my sorority sister, Emily, who would be with her parents in Hawaii for Christmas. Doug was eager to see me and we arranged to meet two days before Christmas. I wondered what it would be like to be with him again. I had experienced so much since I had last seen him in the San Bernardino mountains in August as a Girl Scout counselor. I wondered if he had been as faithful to me as I had been to him.

As my bus pulled into the Greyhound depot, I spotted his tall gangly frame and the familiar blond crew cut. He was waiting at the back of the station, leaning against the battered red Coke machine. I ran to his arms and giggled with delight as he lifted me up and swung me around.

"You don't know how much I've missed you, Doug." I said as we drove to Emily's Glendale home.

"Yeah, well, I've missed you too, Kitten. I want to tell you right now that three months is a long time. You look as blonde and beautiful as ever."

"Were you faithful to me?"

"I have been dating but I've been good. It's just been hard to put up with my father's hassle about us. I don't think he's ever going to let me marry you. He's never gotten over those drunk phone calls from your mother last summer."

"Well, guess what? She's been drunk all over the world being an ugly American, embarrassing me. She even announced to all of First Class coming back to New York that I was a whore. Oh, yeah, and in Bangkok, in an elevator, she called an American guy a 'kike' and attacked him for smoking a cigar."

"You're kidding"

"Now she's in a sanitarium in New Jersey. Merv said she set their house on fire."

"Jesus, Royal, what are you going to do with her?"

"Well, I've asked this priest to help me. You know? The one she's selected to save my soul? What a joke, huh? But he says there is no help in Palm Springs."

"You've really been through a lot, Kitten." Doug reached across the car and pulled me close to him.

"I've missed you so much," I said, closing my eyes and snuggling against his chest. "Tell me what I've been missing at the university. I can't wait to get back there."

"Oh, you missed a wild frat party. We had a Roaring 20's party complete with an old bathtub full of green gin right in the middle of the chapter room. You know the kind of tub, the kind with claw feet?"

"I would have loved wearing a flapper dress but I know you wouldn't have danced the Charleston with me or anyone else for that matter."

"C'mon, Kitten, don't bug me about my dancing."

Doug pulled his old Ford coupe into Emily's driveway.

"You're sure nobody is home?"

"Positive. They are in Hawaii. Look, she sent me the key."

I felt there was a underlying distance that I hoped would soon disappear when we held each other. When we reached Emily's room Doug swept me up into his arms and carried me to the canopied bed. His hands trembled as he untied my hairbow. He slowly unbuttoned my blouse kissing my neck, moving down to my full breasts. Our lips met as my eyes locked into a blue blur. Doug's kisses were tender and loving. The familiar felt safe. I felt him reach between my legs as he moved on top of me. My body froze.

"What are you doing?", I said with alarm.

"I'm not waiting any longer, kitten."

"Stop! You know how I feel about this. You always said you were willing to wait." He continued to press himself against me. I pushed against his flushed chest and struggled to free myself.

"I can't wait," he said.

"Jesus, Doug, get off me. Get off!"

His penis was erect. I leapt off the bed. He grabbed my shoulders and twisted my right arm behind my back, slapping my face with his free hand and forcing me back onto the bed. I struggled and screamed.

"Get—get off me. You promised..."

"There are no more promises," he yelled.

I grabbed his shoulders and pushed with all my might. He forced his body on top of me. His erect penis was on my thigh. He ejaculated immediately.

I rolled over and sobbed into the pillows.

I rode the bus back to Palm Springs on the day before

Christmas. I was enveloped in a cloak of sadness. The future that I had long envisioned would be mine had begun to evaporate. I felt the cold cloud of abandonment creeping over me and I was afraid.

That afternoon, I got a call from Ramona Chandler.

"Hello, honey, I've been thinking about you. Greta told me you were home."

"I'm so glad you called. Did she tell you what happened on our trip around the world?"

"We are sad she broke her sobriety pledge with the Church and that had to happen to you, honey, we really are."

Ramona and Cyril had lived in the desert since the late forties. Cyril was our pharmacist and the owner of the first drug store in Palm Springs. They were our neighbors and my mother had gotten to know Cyril well over the prescription counter.

They had first extended a neighborly welcome to her in nineteen fifty-eight when she was newly arrived in the desert and in the process of building her new house. Mother created a high-security modern marble compound that displayed her paranoia as well as her penchant for Japanese design. She had her name emblazoned in two-and-a-half foot tall brass Japanese characters across the red marble facade of her house. There were no windows. It looked like a mausoleum. So I called it the "The Marble Crypt."

Ramona and I shared the same St. Valentine's Day birthday and as I got to know them she saw something worthwhile in me that made her reach out and draw me into their lives. They called their house "The Enchanted Cottage" and accepted my offer to paint Pennsylvania Dutch style hearts and flowers and trailing vines on their gate, fence, and wooden patio furniture. This project was of major importance to me for two reasons: The Chandlers were trusting me with an artistic undertaking, something my mother had never done and they were opening up their hearts and lives to me, allowing me to spend long hours at their house, getting to know them.

Ramona and Cyril had married at sixteen and eighteen, had never been apart and were still in love. They were self-educated, down-to-earth people who were wholesome and kind, the closest thing I had as role models. Best of all, they saw good in me. If I stayed more than a couple of hours at the Chandlers, my mother would call and in her inimitable way request they send me home as if I were a small child who had over stayed her welcome. I suspected her motive was jealousy.

"My relationship with Doug has failed." I confided.

She was, as always, warm and sympathetic. "Honey, you have so much to offer. You're one of the most beautiful girls I've ever known. Not only on the outside, but your inner spirit. Don't let yourself be depressed by this. If it doesn't work out, then God has something better in store for you. Come and have turkey with us tomorrow. Cyril has made his famous chestnut dressing."

That evening I persuaded Greta to go with me to the Christmas Midnight Mass. St. Theresa's was aglow with candle light and filled with the rich scent of freshly cut pine boughs. We took our seats in a pew near the rear of the crowded church.

Since I hadn't been to confession, I could not receive Holy Communion. Although I was comforted by the familiarity of the ritual, I was also distressed by an internal conflict: I felt guilty about my near rape. On this night in particular, I longed for some solace from my religion but feeling that I was a sinner, I received none.

CHAPTER 2

On the second day after Christmas, Greta and I were alarmed to have our tranquility pierced by a repetitious ringing of the front door chimes. We reached the door simultaneously and opened it to behold my mother in a crumpled gold silk pantsuit with her sun glasses askew, fumbling in her matching gold lizard purse for her house keys. She was drunk. Behind her, an exasperated taxi driver was unloading a single bag from the trunk of the Yellow Cab.

"Mother, what are you doing here?" I cried, floored by her unexpected arrival.

"That's a long story, Royal. Greta, pay the driver one hundred and fifty dollars," she commanded as she lurched through the carved wooden doors.

We looked at the driver in disbelief.

"I brought her all the way from Los Angeles Airport," he explained. "She promised me two hundred dollars, but I'll take one-fifty."

"*Ach, nein,* one hundred and fifty dollars, *mein Gott,* all de vay frum Los Angeles, Madam," Greta mumbled as she disappeared to fetch the money.

The driver handed me my mother's one bag and I wondered what new melodrama had now transpired.

11

"Mother, where is all your luggage?"

My mother poured herself a Scotch, sat down in her antique needlepoint-covered chair in the living room and fitted a filtered Salem into her gold Dunhill cigarette holder. Exhaling a curl of smoke and tapping her hand on the table next to her, she began the account of her recent persecution.

"You'll never believe what I have gone through, Royal. Your brother had me locked up! That S.O.B. put me in a psychiatric ward. They restrained me, Royal! Look at the bruises on my wrists. They took everything away from me, wouldn't even let me have a bobby pin. I demanded to call my lawyer in Chicago."

She angrily twisted the burning end off her cigarette on the side of the ashtray and reached for another.

"A doctor came into my room and called himself a psychiatrist, for Christ's sake. He asked me how I was feeling. He asked me what problem was really bothering me. Can you imagine? I told him he better get good and ready for the problem he was about to have: my lawyer and a big lawsuit."

There was a pause as she stared at nothing in particular. Then she looked at me. "Royal, they took adhesive tape and tagged all my things."

I could imagine my mother's Kent boar bristle brush and tortoise shell combs taped as if she were a child at camp.

"They even taped my name on my wrist. Look at my wrist, Royal, I had a hell of a time getting it off."

I paced the room digesting my mother's rambling story. How did she get her lawyer to spring her out of there? How could she drink again after such a dreadful experience? Didn't being put in a mental institution by her own son shake her up enough to realize she had a problem? Apparently it didn't. I wondered what it would take. I was always wishing for the magic moment, the moment of insight that would turn her around, but now it was hard to imagine what that might be.

With no solution to my mother's drinking in sight, I turned my attention to my own life and how depleted and empty it seemed. I felt an aching void now that my future with Doug looked dark. I looked forward to January when I would be returning to the University of New Mexico and the friendships that had been interrupted by my bizarre trip around the world.

* * *

I readily accepted the escape Father Mike offered me into the glittering social life of Palm Springs. I felt sophisticated and important arriving at country club parties with this dynamic, Irish character whom everybody loved. After the terrible months of shepherding my mother around the world, always on the alert for disaster, it was now a relief and a luxury to get dressed up in my velvet and satin gowns and be squired about on the arm of this dynamic priest.

My mother encouraged me to spend time with him, saying "Maybe he can talk some sense into that thick head of yours." She considered it a victory on her part that I liked Father Mike since she had hand-picked him to save my soul from Doug.

On the Saturday before New Year's I was swimming laps when Greta ushered Father Mike out onto the patio. He was wearing a pair of outlandish Hawaiian bathing trunks, blazoned with swaying yellow and green palm trees.

"Barry Fitzgerald gave me these after he finished "Miracle on 42nd Street," he said, noticing my amusement. "I thought I would just pop by for a dip before I submit myself to the dreary task of hearing confessions."

I smiled to myself knowing that Father Mike's idea of a dip consisted of no more than strolling back and forth in the shallow end while sipping a cocktail. He wouldn't entertain the idea of taking the swimming lessons I repeatedly offered.

He headed for the cabana, saying, "I'm going to create for you another one of my liquid masterpieces. You just stay there in the pool." His impish eyes twinkled. "I'll be bringing it straight away. And hey Greta, you there in the shadows, can I fix you up with one of my specialties, as well?"

Greta, the eavesdropper, was captivated by Father Mike and could never resist spying on his visits. Embarrassed to be found lurking in the patio, she blanched and mumbled, backing toward the house, "*Ach*, no Father, I must help Madam unpack her travel trunks that have come today from New Jersey."

Father Mike emerged from the cabana with two frosty Bloody Marys sprinkled with celery salt and adorned with crisp green celery stalks.

"You drink before you hear confessions, Father Mike?" I asked him as he stepped into the shallow end.

"Ah, now, I believe God knows it will give me a bit more compassion for the sinners," he said, smiling behind his movie-star sunglasses.

I sat on the side of the pool dangling my long, tan legs in the cool water and sipped my Bloody Mary.

"Why is your angel face so clouded today?"

"Oh...I don't know. I'm never going to be able to keep any boyfriends, Father Mike, because my mother always interferes."

Father Mike took off his sunglasses and fixed me with his blue eyes which had now grown serious. "I have talked to your mother about this and I have told her I think you have a fine head on your shoulders, Royal. I have suggested she let you live your own life. You're a grown woman now, and a beautiful one, and you'll be having a life of your own."

He had defended me to my mother? I was stunned. I felt a surge of hope. Maybe this avant-garde priest really could help me.

"Thank you for your vote of confidence," I said. "I really mean it."

I slid into the water and kicked toward the deep end. "Would you like to put your confidence to the test?" I asked him.

"And what might that test be, my dearie darlin'?"

"Let me teach you how to swim."

"I'll just stay right here. I'm content to be watching you, Miss Esther Williams."

CHAPTER 3

A few days later after lunch and martini's at the Ranch Club, Father Mike and I took a drive out into the desert in his shiny black Thunderbird convertible to see the bright new carpet of wild flowers. The winter sun was hot on the desert floor. The snow sparkled on the peaks of the surrounding San Jacinto mountains. As we drove along, I felt a wall of sadness take shape from deep within me, the stones rising up to trap me. Fueled by several martinis, my emotions burst forth and I began to cry.

Father Mike turned off onto a sandy trail and following it some distance into the desert, parked in the shade of a tamarisk tree. By now I was sobbing uncontrollably. Father Mike put his hand on my shoulder.

"There, there, Royal. What could be bothering you so?"

"I think I've had too much to drink. I'm not used to drinking with lunch. I'm a mess." I rubbed my eyes. "Oh, Father Mike, I don't know what to do, my life seems so empty. Terrible things have been happening to me and I don't know why."

"There, there, now, get it all out of you," he said, tenderly patting my shoulder.

"Doug has gone from my life. Maybe if my mother hadn't interfered with Doug's father, maybe Doug wouldn't have done what he did to me. She ruins everything. She doesn't want me to have anyone of my own," I sobbed. "I miss my father. I don't know why he had to die so young and leave me with her. I don't know what to do about her drinking. I'm afraid she's just going to kill herself one way or the other and it will all be my fault."

Father Mike tightened his arm around my shoulder and said, "There, there, Royal, none of it is your fault."

"I know Father Mike, but where am I going to find some help? I believe in God but I have never been able to find any answers in the Church. I tried living like a nun and that didn't work. It just all goes against my nature."

He looked at me and said, "Now, there is nothing wrong with your nature. You are like an angel from heaven, you are."

"No, no, Father. I'm not an angel. Believe me. I am not an angel...I have to tell you something." My throat constricted with dryness. "I must confess my conflict to you here and now, under God, under this desert sky. I can barely say it out loud. I am filled with guilt. I can't help it," I sobbed. "I really loved petting with Doug and I know it seems like I was leading him on, but he shouldn't have, and I know this is a terrible sin. Will my soul truly go to hell for this?" I beseeched him, heavy streams of tears wetting my face.

"He shouldn't have what?"

"I thought he was going to marry me."

"What did he do to you? He didn't..."

"No, no. We never went all the way. But the last time I saw him, he tried to. I wasn't...we haven't ever...we weren't doing anything different. I know I was sinning but he didn't have to attack me that way."

"He attacked you?" Father Mike's face flushed with anger.

"Not exactly. Maybe he thought it was his last chance. His father had forbidden him to see me anymore."

"Not exactly what?"

I became more serious. "I managed to struggle free just in time. It was awful. He promised me, Father. I believed him." I began to cry again.

"That's all right, Royal. There, there. You are safe with me. You know I think the world of you," he offered me his handkerchief.

"How can you think the world of me when I'm surely going to hell for...after all, I partially led him on. I was full of desire. Lust."

Heat waves shimmered off the shiny black hood of the car and the smell of sage brush was strong in the dry air. Father Mike turned toward me, his face was inches from mine. I could feel his breath on my face.

"I have the same problem," he whispered.

That was the end of my confession.

He put his arms around me and drew me to him. I was stunned.

I said, "Father, what are you doing?"

"Royal, priests are not made of stone," he said in a wavering voice. "I am a man and have feelings also." He looked straight into my eyes. "I have a confession for you. I have to confess I'm filled with lust for you. I have been fighting this desire since I first laid my eyes on you, my beautiful angel. You have no idea how I love you, do you?" he said, stroking my hair. "I want to take you in my arms as a man, not a priest, and kiss away the tears that I cannot bear to see clouding those precious blue eyes."

He tilted my chin and began to cover my face with feather light kisses.

"Oh, my God, Father. Oh, my God, can this be happening?" I whispered.

"It's happening and it's beautiful. I've wanted to tell you I love you for so long. Now let me show you."

I clutched my hands to my mouth and my body grew rigid. I felt my tenuous grasp slipping from the banks of reality and the dangerous waters of confusion and alarm roiling up around me.

He gently brushed back my hair and nuzzled my neck.

"That tickles," I giggled.

"But you like it, don't you?," he whispered into my ear. "I want you to tell me all the things you like."

"I'm too shy, Father."

He slowly unbuttoned my blouse. Then slipped my bra strap off my shoulder and kissed my breasts.

"With time, Royal, you won't be shy. With time, my darlin', I'll know you perfectly." He slid his hands under my crinoline petticoat.

* * *

Driving back through the shimmering desert heat, my heart was pounding. Can this be true? What does this older man want with

19

me? Does he really care about me? God, I'm really bombed. Why did I drink all those martinis? Can I go through with this? It feels so good, but it is truly, truly forbidden. Now I'm really going to hell.

We returned to the coolness of the rectory and he led me inside. Father Mike lived in a five-room Spanish-style bungalow that stood opposite the church on a graveled courtyard surrounded by succulents and large cacti. The interior was tastefully decorated with wall-to-wall shag carpeting and blond Drexel furniture accented with pieces of modern art.

Covering one of the living room walls were photographs of Father Mike at various events with the movie stars of his acquaintance. He blithely passed off the attractive decor saying, "Nearly everything you see here is a donation, darlin', tax deductible of course."

Then he came up behind me and encircled me in his arms.

I was shaking all over.

"You're shivering like a little lambkin. I hope it's with passion and not with fear."

"I _am_ afraid, Father Mike. We've been drinking and you're a priest and this is forbidden."

"I am a man first and you are the most extraordinary woman I have ever met and I know this with or without a pitcher of martinis. You are beautiful and talented and I could be happy looking at your face until the very day death comes to fetch me."

He softly kissed the nape of my neck and lightly caressed my buttocks.

I could feel the hard heat of him pressing against me as his breathing grew heavier. He led me down the shadowy hallway to his bedroom. There he took me in his arms and gently started to undress me.

"How smooth your skin is. Like alabaster, it is."

"Will you be gentle with me, Father?"

"As gentle as gentle can be." He kissed the curve of my spine.

I was still shaking with fear and excitement. He eased me down onto the cool satin coverlet of his double bed and explored my body with his tongue. His touch was familiar.

"How can you know me so well?" I could barely speak.

"I know you, Royal. I've always known you."

Breathless and floating on the brink of surrender, I moaned, "Oh, Father Mike, I can't believe this is happening!"

"It is, my angel," he whispered. "It is. And I have but one request."

"What?"

"You've got to quit calling me Father."

After our love-making we lay in bed, our bodies moist with sweat and our arms entwined. I felt peaceful in his arms. The magnitude of what we had done, the accompanying guilt and confusion lay in wait for me in a corner of my mind, but I turned from it and burrowed my head against his chest. Tufts of blond curly chest hair tickled my nose and I took pleasure in his smell.

"I feel so safe in your arms," I said, raising my head to look at him. "But it's just a little weird knowing you're a priest."

"Royal, I'm a man, I am, the same as any other and I didn't make up the celibacy laws."

"But why did you take them?"

"To get out of Ireland," he said.

"What? It can't be as simple as all that."

"Well now, it is. In Ireland, it was the only way for me to leave. I was the youngest of nine children, the last of the litter. Two of my older brothers took over my father's mill and there was really nothing else for me to do. My family had decided that I was the one to be the priest and one of my sisters was designated to be the nun. That's just the way it was."

"You mean you never got a 'calling'?"

"No, there was no calling, it was simply a matter of survival and for me, a way out of Ireland where my life's destiny could only be a dreary and dismal one."

"But then Father Mike..." I stammered. "I mean, listen, I think I would like to call you Father Mike, is that all right?"

"Father Mike it is then, my dearie darlin'," he said tenderly.

"Well then, Father Mike, it's your turn to confess. When did you break your vow of celibacy?"

"In my first parish in New York in the early Thirties . I was fresh from the seminary in Dublin and ah, I still had such a brogue. It was with an Italian woman--she always wore a fancy red dress."

"And there have been others?"

"Many."

"How can you live such a lie?"

"Because I have feelings. I told you I'm not a damned piece of granite."

22

"Then why don't you leave?"

"I have left. Two times."

"You have?"

"Yes, and well-meaning friends told me that they would get me a job. A job be damned! One of them was selling ice-cream contracts. Priests just can't leave and get a job with a recommendation from the Pope, you know."

"What about all your education? All the years of study it took to be a priest?" I asked.

"It was hard work, but that kind of education means nothing in the outside world. Here I make more money than any parish priest in Southern California."

"You talk about the Church as if it were a business."

"It is, my darlin', it simply is and it makes a lot of money. I have created the Shamrock Center, which is my own day-care center that belongs to me, not to the Church, and I have bought some land in San Diego and in Phoenix. So you see now, I have tried to make a life for myself even though I am a priest. I surely cannot rely on the Church for my old age. They don't even have an old people's home for aged, senile priests. How's that for an organization?" he asked bitterly. He reached for his terry-cloth robe and slipping it on, asked if I would like a drink.

"But what about all the other priests, Father Mike?" I called after him as he headed to the kitchen.

He returned with two glasses of champagne on a silver tray.

"Well now, I know for a fact, some are like me, then some are like slabs of granite and some are bloody queers. When I was in seminary at All Hallows in Dublin, I had one attack me in the dormitory. The luck of the Irish!" he said, rolling his eyes.

We sat in bed and sipped champagne. I tried to digest the myriad emotions that surfaced in the wake of making love with a priest. I was attracted to this man, in fact I more than liked this man and he was being honest with me. His revelations about the Church began to explain some of the futility and frustration I had experienced seeking salvation there. The golden Church whose proscriptions so dominated my youth and conflicted with my nature was now showing its tarnished underbelly.

We had both been tricked and trapped. The priest that I drove into the desert with was now beginning to reveal himself as a man and although we were on forbidden ground, his honesty and vulnerability made me trust him more.

"I wish, Father Mike, there was some way I could help you," I said. "Your life seems like such a trap."

"Well now, there is, my beauty." He caressed my lips with his fingers. "You can let me love you."

* * *

The next morning I heard, "Royal, come here. I want to talk with you." I was summoned.

"Just a minute, Mother," I called and grabbed a towel and wrapped it around me. Guilt grabbed at my stomach. Did she know something? We had been so careful. I started to shake as I crossed the marble floor to her dressing room. I looked at her in the mirror.

"Don't drip water all over the floor. Greta just cleaned in

here."

"Okay. What did you want?" I watched her carefully putting on her false eyelashes.

"I just wanted to comment on your character change."

"What character change?" I could feel my knees tremble.

"Damn these things. Why wasn't I born with long lashes?"

"Mother, what character change?"

"Your character change since Father Mike has taken you under his wing."

"Yes?"

"You are so much more courteous and happy. I think you finally might be realizing that sinning with Doug was taking it's toll on you. You know I've always told you, Royal, that whatever you do in life will show up on your face."

I peered into the mirror at my face.

"Yes, look at your face now. It's glowing. A clean life will always make it glow, my darling."

"Glowing." I mumbled.

"I think I will donate another stained glass window to the Church. He is truly doing a good job with you."

I felt the knot in my stomach untie. "Yes, he is quite a good teacher, Mother, and I appreciate your introducing to him. You'll be happy to know that I have forgotten Doug. I'll go back to college with a clean slate."

* * *

Father Mike showered me with attention, calling me every day.

"Are you ready for some serious horseback riding, Royal? You know you are turning into quite an accomplished little equestrian. And should Greta be listening in on the line, please tell that news to Madam immediately."

"Father Mike, you are so insane."

"Would you really be thinking I'm daft, criminally insane of course?"

"I'll be ready at nine sharp."

On these early morning rides, after he said Mass, we thundered across the desert floor and maneuvered our horses up into the coolness of the canyons, hungrily seizing every opportunity for our secret love trysts.

"Tomorrow morning, my darlin', we're going on a picnic," he said, tracing the lines of my face with a feather.

"Father Mike, Father Father Mike, Father Mike. I wish I could call you Father Mike in public," I mused out loud.

"Royal, You know you have to watch yourself at all costs. Nothing must happen to ruin our love." He grew serious.

"Oh, I know that and you know I am careful but sometimes I wish we were free of the beady eyes of Palm Springs society."

"Well, I'll see what I can do to arrange more freedom but in the meantime, get ready for our hike tomorrow. I'll pick you up after I say Mass."

"Are we going to hell for this? Hmmm?" I taunted him.

He slapped me on the butt, "Of course we are. Come now, it's time to mount."

"On the horse?"

In the early morning he picked me up and we drove to Palm Canyon and hiked up the rocky trail to Tahquitz Falls where we made love in the coolness of the palm groves. Afterwards, we were content to lie on our backs and watch the cactus wrens making their nests among the sharp thorns of the prickly cacti.

"Sometimes I feel like nothing more than a court jester." Mike's face looked sad.

"You are a court jester. And very good at your craft. Look at how much money you make for the Church. The letter that Bishop Buddy sent, complimenting you on your collection plate success, should make you proud."

"A business, Royal, like I told you. But, I feel empty. If you were not in my life, I'd be truly lonely."

"Aren't priests supposed to be lonely?"

"Damn it, Royal, I'm a man like any other. Sometimes the shallow and phony social life of this town really eats on me."

"It's not just this town. But I know what you mean. All my life I've felt like a guest in my mother's designer house. I've never fit in. It's almost like I'm an observer, an observer of a family I don't really know."

"Well, no doubt about it, your family has done nothing to perk up your image. Too bad your father had to die so young. Your mother is indeed a sick woman."

"Sick? Yes, indeed, but there are no doctors here to cure her and even if there were, she'd never go to get help. She doesn't think anything is wrong with her. She thinks she is perfectly perfect."

"You're perfectly perfect."

"Don't let her hear that. She thinks you really are saving my soul. It's sort of like living in a cat house. These three women-- one of them me--of different ages mewing around you for your attention. I, of course, being the biggest mewer of them all." I brushed up against him.

"Cat house? Ha...No, those are very dry cats living there. But, not you, no, not you my frisky kitten."

"Don't call me that," I snapped angrily.

"Frisky kitten? Why not?"

"Doug used to call me that. Please don't remind me."

"Now, now, don't think of what was. "Come here," opening his arms to me, "I have a surprise for you."

"You are full of surprises."

"Remember how you wished us to have more freedom?"

"It is my dream."

"Well, how would you like to go on a trip with me?" He smiled.

"How on earth can we go on a trip together?" I looked at him quizzically.

"It is time for my annual trip with the Italianos."

"Those three men from the club who are in the vending and jukebox businesses. The ones you say might be connected with the Mafia?"

"None other. Each year they take me to Las Vegas."
"What for?"

"They include me every year. Maybe they think a priest will bring them good luck with their gambling. Maybe I'm a cover for their wives."

"How on earth can I go along?"

"I've already spoken to your mother."
"You what?" I stared at him.

"I just convinced her that you needed a break. That you would be safe."
"Safe with four men?"

"No, my dearie darlin', three men and a priest. This very priest will be you chaperone."
"She believed you?"

"Of course, and I told her I would be looking after you in the safest manner. You will have a room of your own and I will guard it with my very life."

"What about the other men?"

"They won't notice; they'll be too busy gambling with their whores. Besides, they all think you're beautiful. They'll like your presence."

* * *

My mother was now temporarily on the wagon, had signed another no drinking pledge with the Church and was happy to see me drive off in the custody of this agent of God whom she trusted was redeeming me.

"Royal, I'm taking you to Bullocks to buy some new cocktail dresses. You know these are important men from the club and you must look your very best."

"I can't wait. I saw a royal blue velvet one in the window. Princess style."

"And I will loan you one of my furs," she continued. "It's cold in Las Vegas now. For God's sake, be on your best behavior."

As the private Cessna bounced down the runway, I squeezed Mike's hand.

"You hands are like ice," he said rubbing them briskly.

"I'm afraid if the plane crashes, we'll all go to hell."

"Well, there's one thing for certain," he yelled over the roar of the engines.

"What?"

"You won't be dying without a priest." He laughed merrily.

* * *

Father Mike became my hero. He was the first man in my life who was not afraid to stand up to my mother. After a raging verbal battle with my mother, she called for his help.

"I'm going to call Father Mike and let him hear the way you talk to me, young lady. That sarcastic, smart mouth of yours. I thought you were getting better, but this talk is not acceptable."

"Did you ever hear yourself talk?" I screamed.

"What do you mean, young lady?"

"Did you ever hear yourself when you're drunk?"

"I do not get drunk and I will not tolerate your yelling at me." She straightened her back.

"Oh, yes? You don't get drunk. That's right, you dragged me around the world perfectly sober, right?" I screamed louder.

My mother crossed the room and slapped me across the face.

"That's enough out of you. Greta get me the leather belt."
"You're going to whip me like I was a little kid? I'm not a little kid anymore. I'm twenty years old, for Christ's sake."
"I won't have you swearing either." She slapped me again. "That mouth of yours must be stopped." I winced but stood firmly in front of her.

"You never swear do you? God, I wish we had that tape recording we kids made several years ago when you were <u>drunk</u>. But you erased it, didn't you?"

"I don't know what you're talking about. Get out of my room immediately. Now!"

I slammed the door and ran outside. From the cabana I could hear my mother talking to Father Mike on the phone.

"I thought she was improving, Father, but she is back to her hateful, good-for-nothing self. If you could of heard her just now, taking the Lords name in vain--What did you say? Psychologically harmful? I would suggest you get over here right away and explain that to me in person."

* * *

The wheels of Father Mike's car screeched into the circular driveway. From my hiding place I could see Greta was already holding the ornately carved door open, smirking.

"Madge, really...Let's get this fracas taken care of. Tell me, calmly, your concerns." He rushed into the living room.

"Concerns? You just accused me of doing what you call psychological damage to my daughter, that's what."

Father Mike cleared his throat. "You have done psychological damage to Royal."

"You had better be careful here, Father, be very careful."

"Careful? I am speaking the truth. Did you not take several pledges with the Church for not drinking?"

"What does that have to do with Royal's sarcastic disposition?"

"She has been through a lot with you traveling around the world. Madge, you broke your pledge and she had to pay for that with embarrassment and worry."

"She's never worried in her life. She only thinks about herself."

"Royal worries a lot about you. Maybe too much. She is such a beautiful and artistic young woman, she is. Surely you can recognize that in your own daughter."

"She never worried about me in her life, I said." My mother grew more angry. "I will admit she has a high I.Q. but she has never applied herself...ha, I see now that she has deceived you with her charm. I thought you were helping her, but I see you are not strong enough to deal with her. Greta will show you the way out."

Secretly, I basked in Father Mike's approval and attention.

* * *

"You actually stood up to her!" I can't believe it." I said as we walked our horses.

"So you heard it all? I thought you might me lurking about listening. Your mother is crazy, Royal. It is very hard for me to control myself because I love you so much."

"Yes, I know. She is crazy. You'll never get her to admit to her drinking."

"I feel she is dangerous now. We have to be even more careful."

Suddenly I felt fear. "Well, I understand, but you're not saying that we can't see each other, are you?"

"No, I'm just saying that since I spoke the truth, I'm not playing her game. She will be more suspicious. Just watch yourself now, okay?"

"I would do anything you asked me to," I said.

He drew me into his arms. "Let me kiss away the pain where she slapped you."

* * *

I took it as a sign of Father Mike's confidence in me that he allowed me to choose topics for his sermons. My first topic was: "Charity, Beginning the New Year Right," based on a reading from the book of the prophet Isaiah. I sat in the front pew with my mother and Greta and smiled as Father Mike spoke persuasively to the congregation about the power of charitable deeds. Very soon thereafter, I wrote my first sermon: "Truth and Its Transforming Power," based on a reading from the Acts of the Apostles. My sermons were good. I loved hearing Father Mike deliver them so eloquently from his pulpit and took mischievous delight in the praise voiced by the departing parishioners. I never felt guilty about this, because I knew I had something worth while to say and found I had a knack for presenting the word of God in terms of everyday life.

Father Mike thought so, too. Although he let me write his sermons, and found listening to confessions so painfully repetitious that he took a couple shots of vodka to tolerate them, he never betrayed to me the confidentiality of what he heard there. I respected him for that.

The beginning of the second semester at the university was approaching. I felt as though I had lived through an entire lifetime in the past year. I had traveled far from the San Bernardino Mountains where, last summer, so carefree, I had taught rock cookery to my eight-year-old Girl Scout campers. I had taken a roller coaster ride through a kaleidoscope of cultures and looked into the helpless eyes of bony beggars in Calcutta. And now my mind reeled from the intimate exposé of the Catholic Church and the implications of my involvement with Father Mike. How was I ever going to fit back into the Chi Omega sorority house?

CHAPTER 4

After three weeks of intimacy with Father Mike, I missed my period. I went to a phone booth and called him.

"Father Mike, I have to meet with you immediately."

"Is it your mother again, my dearie darlin'?"

"No, this is really important. Where can we meet?"

"I'll be done with confessions at four o'clock. Meet me in my church."

"In your church? Won't people see us?"

"Maybe, but it will look official."

Father Mike was still in the confessional box when I arrived that afternoon. I took a seat in a back pew. When Father Mike finally came out, he found me on my knees crying.

"What can it be, Royal? What's troubling you so?" he whispered as he kneeled beside me.

"I think I'm pregnant." I sobbed.

"What? How can that be?"

"I don't know...those suppository things you got didn't work. What am I going to do, for God's sake? It's bad enough living with my mother, let alone this. What are we going to do, Father Mike?"

"We're going to get you checked by a doctor in Redlands. That's what we're going to do first."

* * *

I had regular periods all my life and I knew my body functioned like clockwork. I knew I was pregnant but went along with Father Mike to meet the doctor. As we drove, I told him that I was terrified by the thought that I was pregnant, let alone with the child of a priest.

"You don't know that for sure yet. Please don't talk about it anymore until we get the test done," he snapped at me.

I sat wrapped in a cocoon of icy silence.

"Remember you are a married woman named Betsy Ryan from Upland, whom I am helping. Let me hear you say your lines."

* * *

An hour later, a tight-lipped nurse led me into the gynecologist's drab office.

"Take off your clothes, there's a gown behind that screen for you to put on. Then get up on the table and wait for the doctor."

This was the first pelvic exam of my life. I felt nervous and embarrassed. The doctor strode into the small room. The nurse handed him powdered rubber gloves which he put on.

"Mrs. Ryan? Yes, well, please move your buttocks down toward the end of the table." I inched my way to the bottom of the paper covered table. My knees were locked together.

"Would you please separate your legs? I won't be able to examine you if you don't." He placed a cold metal speculum inside of me. My knees were shaking.

"I'm just going to check your uterus. You will feel some pressure." He said pushing on my lower stomach. "You've given your urine sample to the nurse?" I nodded. "Okay, that will be all. You can get dressed now."

* * *

A week later Father Mike called me at home to meet with me. He had received the test results.

"Well, yes or no?" I asked over the phone.

"It is best that I pick you up."

The sun was setting behind the peaks of San Jacinto, creating fingers of dark shadows across the desert. We drove out toward Desert Hot Springs.

"The answer is yes. You are with child." Father Mike sighed.

"Yes? I am pregnant? I told you I was pregnant, Father Mike. You made me go through all that charade for nothing."

"We had to make sure, Royal. But, God will send us a solution."

"God? You think God will give us a solution? I'm pregnant with the child of a Catholic priest who wouldn't practice birth control and God is going to help us out?" I grew angry.

Father Mike reached over and squeezed my hands. "I know this is hard for you, Royal. You must remember that I love you."

"I love you too, but now we've gone beyond the limits. With a mother like mine? Do you want to see me killed?"

"Your mother must never know about this." He frowned.

"She won't, believe me, she won't. I have another idea, Father Mike." I could feel my heart racing.

"And what might that be?"

"Well, Zibby Katz, my friend in high-school, had an abortion in Chicago. I could get an abortion if we could figure out some way to get me to Chicago."

Father Mike was horrified. "Abortion? Did you say abortion?"

"Yes, it would solve everything. It's a Michigan Avenue doctor, Father Mike. Zibby told me all about it. She walked in and walked out all in one morning. It cost $400.00."

"How can you talk like this? How can you be thinking like this, Royal?"

"I don't want you trapped into anything with me. This way no one would ever know."

"God will know."

"There you go again with God. Has God told you how to handle this one, Father Mike? What has God said to you? He hasn't said a thing to me!"

"I won't hear any more of this talk."

"What do you mean? We have to talk. This is my life, my body. This is your life as a priest that is threatened. We have to talk."

"How can you talk about murdering our very own child?" he responded with alarm. "I am older than you and I want to have this child."

"You want to have our child? It's me who's having this baby. And anyway, I don't believe it's murder, Father Mike. I don't want us trapped in a situation that we will be sorry for later. I love you, but this is serious!"

"Yes, very serious, and it has to be handled very carefully."

"For God's sakes, Father Mike, don't say to me you want me to go into one of those homes for unwed mothers and then give up the baby. I'd rather die. I couldn't go through that, I just couldn't, so let me save my sanity and let me save you as a priest, let me go to Chicago!"

"No, I am going to marry you," he said softly.

"You want to marry me? How can you do that?"

"I've been thinking about our situation for a long time. I love you, Royal. I am sick of living fraudulently. I want to set this straight with God and everyone else. I'm going to leave the priesthood and I'm going to marry you. But I have to tread carefully. It will take some time and doing, but this is my decision and I don't want to hear another word about abortion. I am responsible. I have been thinking about this day and night. I am happy you are pregnant. Please, trust me."

I couldn't believe Father Mike loved me that much. He wanted me, he even wanted my child. Father Mike loved me for who I really was. I felt valued. I had no idea how he would arrange our lives outside the dominion of the Roman Catholic Church or the far-reaching tentacles of my mother's fury, but I put myself in his hands and let him take command. Surely God couldn't condemn him for finally being honest with himself.

"You know this isn't going to be easy for us, my precious. It's going to be a hard road and there'll be insults to bear. There will be no more country clubs or fancy living. You'll have to give up a lot of what you're used to, to be the wife of Father Mike Raymond O'Donohoe."

"I can take it, Father Mike. I am aware of what's to come but we have each other and a love that's so rare. I know what will happen on my side. My mother will disinherit me and God knows the rest of my family and friends will disown me. But I love you. You'll see: I'll be strong for you."

"This is serious, Royal. I mean it. It's going to be a hard road." His brow was furrowed, his face tense.

"I will be happy to live a simple life with you, Father Mike Raymond O'Donohoe. It will be a new life; we'll burn all our bridges. As for the hypocrisy of life here in Palm Springs, I can't wait to get out of it. I can't wait for our love to be out in the open."

Father Mike's plan was to support us on his income from the Shamrock Center, his nursery school for Catholic working mothers. This income would be augmented by the monthly repayment of a $10,000 loan to an old Air Force buddy of his named Harold White.

"So long as Mrs. Sullivan sends us my check each month from the Shamrock Center, we'll be able to live comfortably. But we'll have to leave the country at first until things simmer down," Father Mike said.

"You mean México?" I asked.

"God no. Your mother would find us in no time and cause a riot. I mean someplace in Europe. We'll have to do some research. I figure if we stay away for a year or two things with your mother and the Church will have simmered down enough for us to return."

We decided that I would return to school while Father Mike finalized the plans for "our Exodus," as he called it. He had to get the Shamrock Center in order and since his assistant priest was being transferred to another parish, he had to find someone to take over when he handed in his resignation.

Before I left for University of New Mexico, Father Mike wanted me to go with him to see a lawyer. To protect himself from possible allegations that he had abducted me out of the country against my will, he had a lawyer draw up a statement for me to sign. I realized then, that I could be crossing a dangerous line.

* * *

My mother started to become suspicious of our relationship when Father Mike stood up in my defense. One evening in her crypt-like living room, during a discussion about my return to college, she commented, "Royal doesn't have a brain in her head, she has the judgment of a jackass. I just hope she doesn't take up again with that stupid boy from Santa Barbara who will only end up as a good-for-nothing truck driver."

I saw Father Mike flinch and a flush of anger cross his face.

"Will you listen to yourself now, Mrs. Phillips," he said. "Your daughter's not daft. She seems to have a good head on her shoulders and I bet she knows what she's doing. She's got your blood in her, doesn't she now?"

It had never occurred to my mother that Father Mike would often disagree with her viewpoint of me. She had chosen him to do her bidding in regard to me. She had thought of him as a loyal ally and was now surprised and angered by his signs of defection. No longer confident that this priest was saving my soul, she was anxious for me to return to school. Father Mike and I sensed this shift in her and became more cautious about covering our tracks.

After making love one evening in the rectory just a few days before my departure, Father Mike and I took a walk through the deserted church garden in the still night air. The only sounds were the gravel crunching beneath our feet and the coyotes' familiar howl, echoing off the mountains.

Father Mike stopped, tilted my head toward him, and kissed me softly. "I know what we will name her," he said.

"Her? How do you know this baby is a girl?" I asked.

"Because I know. And she will be as bonny and beautiful as you are," he said, wrapping his arms around me and hugging me close to him. "We will name her Dierdre."

"And what might that name be meaning, Father Michael Raymond O'Donohoe?" I asked.

"Dierdre was a princess with hair of gold in a Celtic legend."

"I wonder what kind of life our princess will have," I said, thinking about the uncertain path ahead of us.

"She may be subjected to suffering because of our circumstances but if we raise her right, it will strengthen her. Will you come to the car with me now?" he asked. "I have a surprise for you."

I got into the car and Father Mike asked me to close my eyes and put out my hands. I felt him place a paper bag in them. I squeezed it. It was soft and squishy.

"Can I open my eyes now?"

"Just as long as there is a sparkle in them and you do something great with your talents," he said.

I peered into the bag. "Pink yarn! You beautiful, beautiful man."

Packing my trunks for the University of New Mexico was a difficult and emotional undertaking. I knew I would not be returning again to Palm Springs before Father Mike and I left the country.

* * *

Father Mike had gotten books and brochures for us about Spain, Portugal, the Canary Islands off the coast of Africa and the island of Madagascar, in the Indian Ocean. We were looking for a destination civilized enough for me to safely deliver Deirdre and far enough away to foil my mother's attempts to find us.

* * *

I sifted through my old records, my yearbooks, my photo albums, my boxes of old dance bids, realizing that I was packing for what might be the rest of my life. How much of my old life could I put in a trunk. Or even want to put in a trunk?

With our secret plan in my heart, I arrived back at school at the end of January for spring semester. I moved back into the sorority house and went through the motions of attending classes and chapter meetings. Father Mike would alert me when everything was ready. I hoped that would be before my baby started to show.

My sorority sister, Christine, was my only confidant. She was alarmed and worried that I was pregnant and about to run off with a forty-eight year old Catholic priest, but she stood by me in spite of her misgivings and I knew I could trust her. Several times, Father Mike flew both of us to meet him in Phoenix so that he and I could spend the weekend together. Christine knew she was my cover and enjoyed the trips. Slowly over the course of these weekends with Father Mike and me, she changed her mind. She grew very fond of Father Mike and began to believe in the depth of our love. In the end she supported our plans and was relieved that I would finally be free from my mother.

Father Mike wrote me long, eloquent letters nearly every day. It was as if our separation now allowed us an extended courtship. Our whirlwind beginning was digested and strengthened through a stream of letters back and forth in which we expressed our fears, our hopes and our dreams for a future together. Father Mike told me he had seen my mother at Thunderbird Country Club and she was sober for once. "You know, when I was talking to her," he wrote, "I wanted so much to tell her how I love you. I can't believe someone as lovely as you came out of such a dreadful woman. I daily fear the trouble she could make if she finds out about us before we leave the country."

The heavy shroud of deceit that had surrounded Father Mike's life for so long was becoming intolerable now that he had made his final decision to leave the Church. He felt as if he were suffocating and he was going through the preparations for our departure frantically like a man trapped in a grave who senses the presence of fresh air above him. Through these letters I began to glimpse the core of this man and I loved him more. And every week there were flowers. He also sent me money to buy maternity and baby clothes for my trunk.

True to form, my mother began making drunken calls to the sorority house, usually late at night. Since Father Mike had defended me, he was now a target and many of her calls included a whining criticism of his lack of respect for a mother's worries.

"What kind of priest would defy a mother's judgment about her own daughter?" she would drunkenly whine.

Once she designated him an enemy, she leveled all kind of wild accusations at him and some came frighteningly close to the truth. She had heard some gossip about his philandering from her masseuse and this fueled her attack. I let Father Mike know that he was now on her black list and warned him to be wary of her. I had Christine intercept most of her phone calls and tried to avoid having to talk to her at all.

I longed to begin my life in the open, and I too, was struggling with my charade. My recent travels had taken me beyond the frivolity of campus life and the fact that I was now carrying the child of a Catholic priest further alienated me from the conventional.

I had Father Mike's photograph in a silver frame on my bureau and when my sorority sisters asked, "Is that your father?" I would say, smiling, "You could say that."

I was knitting pink baby blankets during my sorority chapter meetings, but no one seemed to notice or think it was strange. It was at this very time that the editor of the LOBO, our college paper, wanted to honor me by featuring me as "campus cutie," a sort of apple-pie pin-up of the week. I marveled at the irony.

Father Mike flew to Albuquerque on Valentine's Day for my twenty-first birthday. He brought with him a book on the Canary Islands which he had decided would be the best destination for us. "It is off the coast of west Africa," he said. "We can live cheaply there, and if it doesn't work out, we can go to Spain. When we land in London we will get married and then take the boat to Las Palmas de Gran Canaria."

"Sounds great to me, Father Mike. When do we leave?" I asked.

"It will take me until April, I fear, to get the finances of the Shamrock Center squared away and my replacement groomed. I can't announce my resignation until everything is in order. For me, my love, tomorrow couldn't be too soon and I know this waiting is hard for you, too. I know it isn't easy pretending everything is 'Sally-coed.'"

After my birthday dinner at La Hacienda in Old Town, Father Mike presented me with a little heart shaped cake. "I want you to be eating the whole cake now," Father Mike said, his blue eyes twinkling.

"The whole cake? No! You have some too, Father Mike," I protested.

"No no, there's an Irish tradition taking place here, my dearie darlin', the whole cake is for you."

While Father Mike watched me, I began to eat the little cake glazed with pink and white flowers.

"Mmm, Rum cake. My favorite," I said. "You remembered."

Father Mike just smiled and kept his eyes on me. I felt the ring in my mouth on the second to the last bite. Father Mike was laughing delightedly as I spit it out into my hand. It was a gold wedding band.

"Read the inscription," Father Mike urged.

I licked away the icing and through my tears I read. "TO R, MY LOVE FOR ALWAYS, MOD."

Father Mike and I discussed whether or not I should go to a doctor. I felt confident everything was okay. Just as he was convinced I was having a girl, I was convinced my pregnancy would progress normally. I saw no need to see a doctor and risk anyone finding out I was pregnant.

CHAPTER 5

Two weeks after my twenty-first birthday, I was summoned to a downtown church in Albuquerque to be interrogated by a panel of priests sent by Bishop Buddy to investigate Father Mike's actions in Palm Springs. Rumors about Father Mike and me had grown as they do in small towns where people hungrily feed on morsels of gossip that take their attention away from themselves and their petty problems. Palm Springs society relished this snack about their favorite Catholic priest.

Father Mike and I had always been guarded about showing anything other than friendship in public but someone must have seen something.

When my mother got drunk she indulged her habit of creating long distance havoc by calling Bishop Buddy, the bishop of Southern California, to inform him of her own suspicions regarding Father Mike. God only knows what she said to him but it must have added momentum to the rumors. He had sent the Chancellor of the Diocese to Albuquerque to determine the truth of all these rumors. Before the investigation, I tried to call Father Mike but I couldn't reach him. I put on a flowered Lanz dress with a high lace collar and cuffs and I went to face them straight on to show that I had nothing to hide. Christine drove me.

The meeting took place in the side chapel of the Cathedral in downtown Albuquerque. I sat alone in a wooden chair opposite a council of six, four priests in black cassocks and two church lawyers in dark business suits. When I saw the lawyers, I guessed that my mother had been sharpening her accusations with her usual threats of a law suit. The Church was now forced to investigate the possibility that their popular and profitable priest might be a detriment to their organization.

Father Mathews, the Chancellor in charge of the interview, explained that there had been serious accusations of impropriety against Father O'Donohoe which they wished to question me about. They said, "Father O'Donohoe was reported driving with a blond woman in the desert. Were you that woman? Father O'Donohoe was seen on the Palm Canyon trail with a young blond woman."

My stomach began to tighten and my hands turned to ice. I sat there under fire and my mind raced. My loyalty to Father Mike was so fierce, I would have killed for him. So I sat there and I lied through my teeth. I lied easily with my eyes looking right into theirs.

"No," I answered calmly. "No, I've never been to the desert with Father O'Donohoe. He has been a friend and a counselor to my family and he frequently comes over to our house. He often attends parties at our country club. I've sought his advice about my mother's drinking problem."

The lawyers asked a few questions about my mother's "drinking problem," in response to which I answered that she sometimes went on binges and was not responsible for her actions, which worried me and my brother a great deal. They said they wanted to ask me some questions about Father O'Donohoe's social behavior at the country clubs. Did he often dance? Did he dance with me?

Without hesitation I answered, "Why, of course. He is a marvelous dancer. He has danced with me and my mother many times. Mrs. Bogert, the mayor's wife, always dances with him. In fact, my last image of Father O'Donohoe is of him whirling eighty-four-year-old Mrs. Riordan all over the dance floor at Thunderbird's Christmas Ball."

My willingness to answer their questions seemed to pacify them. I thought I perceived a flicker of relief on Father Mathew's face.

Riding back up to the campus with Christine, I reflected on the fabulous gift my mother had given me. I had her to thank for the presence and composure I had developed over years of smoothing over her outrageous public faux pas. When I finally reached Father Mike on the phone that night and told him about the investigation, he was alarmed, though he praised me for remaining level-headed. He thought the fact that my mother made her accusations to the Archbishop at two o'clock in the morning while drunk cast doubts on her credibility, which would now become a point in our favor.

Nevertheless, he agreed we had to get moving out of the country soon. The situation was becoming unbearable for both of us.

CHAPTER 6

Father Mike called me on the morning of March twenty-third to say he was ready. He had finalized monthly arrangements to receive the money that we would live on. Mrs. Sullivan, his secretary and only confidant, would collect the monthly loan payment from Harold White and send it together with the profit from the Shamrock Day Care Center. Father Mike had written his resignation and instructed her to mail it to the Archbishop on the Monday after Easter.

Our departure would coincide with spring break at UNM. I told my mother I was going to spend the vacation at Christine's home in Abilene, Texas. I asked her to call me there on Easter Sunday, April 2, so we could wish one another a happy Easter. But by then we would be safely in England and Christine would tell her I had left with Father Mike. No one, at this point, knew our destination, so Christine could truthfully say she didn't know. I flew to Los Angeles to meet Father Mike. I shipped my trunk to California from New Mexico to the home of Harold White who would secretly harbor us until our departure from the United States. Father Mike and Harold had met each other in the Air Force during the war, while Father Mike was serving as chaplain.

My trunk contained my newly purchased maternity clothes from J.C. Penney's, the baby blankets I had knitted, one <u>Better Homes and Gardens Cookbook</u>, all the things I felt important and necessary to begin my new life with Father Mike and our love-child.

The plane to Los Angeles was filled to capacity with Easter vacationers. I spotted Father Mike's face in the crowd of people meeting the plane. He was grinning from ear to ear.

"Here's my Royal O'Donohoe," he said, wrapping his arms around me and squeezing me. "And what a splendid day it is to be startin' a new life."

"Oh, Father Mike, I'm so relieved to be out of there! We're almost on our way. I couldn't stand pretending anymore," I said, leaning my head against his shoulder as we made our way out of the terminal.

On the one-and-a-half hour drive to Redlands we discussed our plans for the week. We would be staying with Harold and his family, doing last-minute errands and packing before our departure on the Monday after Easter.

I had never seen Father Mike looking so happy. He had only taken the first steps away from the lies of his old life and already he seemed lighter. This was a sign to me that the radical choices we had made were correct. That night I fell asleep in his arms feeling serene and complete.

After a long day of last-minute shopping on Thursday, we sat down to a candlelight dinner with the White family in their Spanish-style dining room. The phone rang. It was Christine calling from Texas.

"Royal, your mother knows! She's drunk and she's been calling here all day long. I don't know what you're going to do but

I had to tell her. Royal, I'm so sorry. She called last night when I wasn't here. She was so drunk and she got my mother who said she didn't know where you were and after that, she just kept calling."

"Oh, my God, Christine! What did you tell her?" I asked in a panic.

"I told her what we had planned, that you had gone away with Father Mike, but I didn't know where. She was screaming that he was going to sell you into white slavery. She just went crazy! She said she was going to call your brother and some family lawyer and the FBI. Royal, I'm really worried that she is going to find you."

"You didn't tell her where we are now, did you?"

"Of course not," she reassured me. "I didn't tell her anything! I said I didn't know where you went."

"God, Christine, we're going to have to somehow accelerate our plans to get out of here. I'll have to talk to Father Mike. I'm so sorry for all the trouble I've caused you and your family. We'll let you know where we are when we get settled somewhere and listen, Christine, if she calls again, just don't tell her anything. And Christine, pray for us!"

I hung up the phone and returned to the dining room ashen white. Father Mike took one look at my face and excused himself from the table.

During the next twenty-four hours Father Mike did everything in his power to get us on an earlier flight to London. My adrenaline was running high but I recognized this was not a new sensation. I had become used to being terrified. Because it was Easter weekend, all the airlines were heavily booked. Father Mike finally managed to get us on a standby list for Friday night. We were afraid to wait in the airport for so long, but we had no choice.

We piled our luggage near the Pan Am ticket counter and while Father Mike paced back and forth, continuously mopping his brow, I scanned the crowd, expecting any minute to see my brother or my mother's lawyer coming toward us. At the very last minute, they called out our names. I felt as if we were moving in a dream. We rushed forward with our luggage and within minutes we were aboard the plane. The heavy metal doors were pulled shut behind us.

"We made it darlin'," Father Mike said, mopping his forehead as the plane lifted off. "One of the hardest parts is over. I think I'm going to pass out."

We ordered vodka and tonics and toasted our new life.

CHAPTER 7

In London, Father Mike had arranged for us to stay at an enchanting bed and breakfast inn near Kew Gardens. At each meal, there was a flower on my plate that Father Mike had somehow managed to materialize. At dinner, he remembered my favorite wine, Liebfraumilch, and for dessert, he introduced me to rum trifle. Father Mike indulged in his favorite meal: English mixed grill, which consisted of lamb chops, sausage, chicken livers, veal kidney and bacon with grilled tomatoes and mushroom caps and onions basted in clarified butter. I was amazed that he could digest such a mixture.

He knew London well and gallantly ushered me on a tour of its sights including a ride on the red double-decker buses. In the evening we went to a stage play where I was surprised and delighted to have hot tea served to us in our seats.

It was raining the day we had chosen to get married. Father Mike wore a gray suit and vest and bought me a little nosegay to match the blue silk suit which had been made for me in Hong Kong while there with my mother. We wanted a simple and quick civil ceremony. When we went to the registry office to get our marriage license we were told by the official that we had to reside in England for two weeks in order to get the license. When Father Mike protested, he was told the only way around the wait was to send a petition to the Bishop of Canterbury. The thought of petitioning a bishop, even an Anglican one, sent Father Mike's handkerchief nervously to his brow.

"Our ship is leaving for the Canary Islands in three days so we won't be able to get married here. We'll have to get married there. Do you mind terribly?" he asked, as he put his arm around me.

"I'm disappointed, but I guess there's nothing else we can do. I just want this ring on my finger to be real," I said, touching the gold wedding band he had given me months before.

We left for the Canary Islands from South Hampton on the "Pretoria Castle," a Royal British mail steamer bound for Africa. True to English tradition, she was an elegant ship whose social activities included captain's cocktail parties and tea dances. Father Mike and I made friends wherever we went. People were drawn to us. We both had a sense of humor and although I often felt very shy, I was poised, and, like Father Mike, I was a good story teller and I had a lot of material to draw from.

Father Mike had devised a cover story about himself composed of half-truths. He was in "real estate" in California and had now come to Europe to write a book. He held court with the guests at the Captain's first cocktail party, holding them spellbound with details of his proposed novel, which he told them was about the adventures of an Air Force Chaplain in the Korean war. He went so far as to tell them that his main character had the delightful duty of tagging dead soldiers' toes and collecting their personal articles.

Later, I asked him, "Is that something you really did in the Air Force, Father Mike?"

"Yes, that and get into trouble," he said.

"And you got the scar on your back then?"

"Yes."

"Tell me how."

"I told you, I got it in the war."

"I know, but how?" I asked.

"Running away from the enemy," he said, smiling broadly.

"Father Mike, you're never serious and I never know when to believe you. You're the king of con-artists and I'm too gullible."

"Oh, yes, you're very gullible, you are, Royal O'Donohoe," he said, swatting my bottom. "And dumb like a fox!"

CHAPTER 8

After three days of calm seas and gala parties, we landed at the port of Las Palmas on the island of Gran Canaria. The destination we had chosen was not at all what we had hoped. Las Palmas was a large oil bunkering port with few attractions. We soon got "islanditis" and agreed that Gran Canaria was too expensive, full of other runaway Americans and disappointment. We flew to the neighboring island of Tenerife where we met an American couple en route to Spain. She was a professor of home economics at the University of Puerto Rico on her way to the culinary archives in Spain to do research for a book. They spoke enthusiastically about the charm of Southern Spain and eagerly gave us pointers on where to go. Since we had found nothing to our liking in Tenerife, Father Mike and I decided to go to Spain.

We booked first-class passage to Cadiz with the Compania Transmediterrania Española on an old wooden ship that looked like a remnant of the Spanish Armada. She was tiny and her first-class port holes didn't open. There was no ventilation. At times I felt I couldn't breathe. All the rooms had narrow bunk beds, so in order to sleep next to each other, we had to drag the heavy cotton mattresses onto the floor at night and replace them each morning. To cheer me, Father Mike referred to this as wall-to-wall bedding.

There were hundreds of canary birds in little, makeshift, wooden cages which were stacked up to the ceiling in the hallways outside of the rooms. Nestled at the top of the narrow wooden stairway connecting the lower and upper decks swayed a brightly colored tempera Madonna. The Spanish Army had recruited fifty soldiers from the Canary Islands for service in Seville, and, consistent with the Spanish disregard for capacity limits, their numbers exceeded accommodations. The problem was solved by bedding them down on the open first-class deck. To reach a deck chair I had to pick my way through a sea of sprawling soldiers. Sometimes a group of them would whistle at me and make suggestive movements with their hips.

As the skies darkened and the seas grew turbulent, I began to worry.

"Father Mike, do you think this antique vessel will make it to Spain?"

"It looks like it's going to take a little longer with the sea being this rough, but don't worry your noggin'. Just get as much fresh air as you can. It'll be good for you and my little Irish princess."

As the seas churned and tossed our ship about, fewer and fewer people showed up at the captain's table for meals, until finally, the captain himself ceased to appear. A journey of three days had now stretched to seven and we had run out of food. The crew was catching fish for the galley to fry. Fortunately, very few people were up to eating. I continued to take Father Mike's advice to stay in the fresh air and it seemed to work. I was surrounded by miserable soldiers retching over the rails. One by one the other passengers had turned green and taken refuge below. Father Mike and I were the only ones still standing.

"Did you see all those people barfing over the railing as we came up? And the soldiers huddled together like cattle?" I said to Father Mike as we climbed the companionway to the upper deck. "I feel so sorry for them. Everyone but me is sick, except for you, that is."

"Yes, for a pregnant little wifey, you're a superb traveler," he said, turning from me to clutch the rail.

"What are you doing, Father Mike? Where are you going?" I watched him lurch forward and retch over the side of the ship.

CHAPTER 9

We landed in Cadiz four days behind schedule. From Cadiz we took a train inland to Seville.

"Father Mike," I said, "are you aware that my passport has just expired? Will I get into trouble here?"

"I've been thinking about that. It may just be an opportunity."

"An opportunity for what?"

"An opportunity to get your mother off your back."

"My mother?"

"She must have someone trailing us. I wouldn't put it past her. I told you we'd have to be very careful to cover our tracks so she can never find us."

"Sounds scary. What do you want me to do?"

"Well, since we're not married yet, let's pretend we are."

"And?'

"And all you have to do is go to the American Embassy with your expired passport and say that you have recently married. You ask for a new one in your married name. We're going to get married soon anyway so it would save a lot of trouble of changing it again."

I sighed. "I can't wait for us to be legally married."

"Do you see my point?" he said.

"Yes, but isn't that against the law?"

"Yes, but not to worry, because, we will be married soon."

I thought of all the arched eyebrows we had encountered at the hotel desks when we registered with different surnames. It would be a feeling of relief to hand them passports of the same name.

Before we entered the American Embassy in Seville, Father Mike and I had practiced what I was going to say. I was nervous, but determined. Shoulders squared, I marched through the arched mosaic tiled entry way and into the passport office. Ready to master the Embassy counsel I was affronted by a menacing guard motioning me to the end of a long line of twenty people.

As I shifted from foot to foot, I could feel my confidence dwindle with each minute I had to wait. I was starting to shake by the time the counsel official abruptly said, "Next."

"Good morning, sir. I'm here to renew my passport."

"Ah...yes. Are there any changes?" he asked.

"Yes, um...if you'll look at my papers, you'll see that I've married and have a new name."

"You'll need your marriage certificate." he said impatiently. "Do you have it with you?"

"No! It's at home in the United States. It's in our...our safety deposit box with the rest of our important papers." I stammered.

"I can't issue you a new one without your marriage certificate."

"But, wait...it isn't something you travel abroad with, is it?" I held my breath.

He looked me in the eye and then agreed, "No, of course not. Your signature on this document will be your oath that you are married and that this is your legal name. Sign here."

My heart was pounding as I signed my new name. I could breathe again. When I turned around, I could see Father Mike standing in the marble foyer, mopping his brow with his linen handkerchief. Now I was Royal O'Donohoe, but still unmarried.

CHAPTER 10

From the moment we decided to go to Spain, Father Mike had talked enthusiastically about going to the bullfights. He had often driven down to see this spectacle in San Luis on the Arizona-México border with the Mayor and his wife and other bullfight aficionados from Palm Springs. They always came back loaded with mementos and gory tales of *la hora de verdad*, the moment of truth in the bullring. Now Father Mike said he would be able to attend a bullfight in one of the world's most renowned bullrings, the Maestranza de Sevilla. On Sunday, we took a taxi to the Paseo de Colón and merged into the pressing crowd of black-clad spectators that streamed into the arena. We took our seats high in the stands overlooking the immaculate, raked sand arena. I immediately thought of the Roman Coliseum and the bloody gladiatorial combats of ancient times.

A burst of trumpets heralded the matador's entrance from the dark corridor into the brilliant sunlit arena. The cheering crowd came to its feet. The matador circled the arena, strutting like a peacock, his arms held high in salutation to the crowd. The intricate gold threads of his jacket glistened in the blazing sun. I could see by the enthralled look on Father Mike's face that he was already lost in this spectacle and beyond explaining it to me. When the bull, bleeding and enraged by the barbed *banderillas* that were stuck in his shoulders, lunged at the padded flanks of the picador's horse, Father Mike cringed and became angry.

"This is the only part I hate," he said, his face reddened with heat. "It's not fair to the horses; I can't bear to see the horses hurt."

I knew that Father Mike had horses of his own, but I thought it curious that now all similarity between horse and bull was lost in this cruel ballet. Were not horse and bull both full of fear and hurting? The crowd screamed "Olé" with each pass of the matador's scarlet cape, as he side-stepped closer and closer into the path of horns. The graceful motions of the splendidly costumed matador in his pink stockings and black ballet-like slippers belied the violence at the heart of this ceremonialized dance of death. A stillness fell over the crowd as the matador arched his back, lunged forward into his final pass and sank his shiny sword into lower neck, piercing the heart of the already weakened bull. The bull sank to his knees and with a timeless expression of defeat and surrender, raised his glazed eyes to the sky. Then he slowly lowered his head as rivulets of blood oozed over his protruding tongue. I felt the roar of the crowd pulling me back from the hypnotic intensity of the kill, from the soundless chamber I had been drawn into watching this terrifying *hora de verdad*. I came back with the cheering crowd that now stomped and waved their white handkerchiefs wildly. Father Mike was bathed in sweat and had jumped to his feet to applaud the matador. As the matador circled the ring acknowledging the crowd and basked in the thundering ovation, three *jinetes* on horseback lassoed the bull carcass and dragged it away leaving a trail of blood in the yellow sand. Next a group of *limpiadores* entered on foot and cleaned away the blood-stained sand with their rakes and shovels. Now the purity of the arena was reestablished for the next fight.

I felt the sun beating down on the back of my neck and smelled the pungent odors of the excited humanity around me. I reflected on how easily the stains had been removed by the *limpiadores* so like the Catholic ritual of confession where the soul is wiped clean by absolution. I reflected on the image of my own soul which, surely, by now, from living in sin and being pregnant by a Catholic priest, was densely dotted with black stains, a corrupt Pointillism of the soul.

Father Mike was starving after the bullfights. We found a simple tavern on a narrow street near the Plaza del Salvador that served the traditional *paella* a saffron-flavored rice dish, as its *menú del día*. Father Mike ordered a Sangría and we ate at a small outdoor table where the usual ensemble of starving cats positioned themselves at our feet and mewed. It made me nervous to be surrounded by so many cats staring at us with their unflinching gaze, at the same time I felt pity for them. Father Mike was annoyed by their pleading presence and kicked at them.

"Father Mike, please don't hurt them, they're starving."

He again took aim with his foot. "There are too damn many of them, Royal. It's a damn bother the way the Spanish let them multiply. You're such an infant at times. I should think you'd be more a bit more toughened up having been around the world and back with your crazy mother."

"Yes. True I'm twenty eight years younger than you- an infant if you like, but I have feelings for these animals."

"You'll be learning as you get older," he sighed wearily.

The waiter brought us our *paella.*

"I think we should visit Granada before we come back to the coast to find a place to live," Father Mike said as we ate. "I want you to see that beautiful city."

"Where is it?" I asked.

"It's east of here on a mountain plain surrounded by the snowcapped peaks of the Sierra Nevada. We can take a train."

Then he burst into a few loud strains of the song, "Granada." I giggled and the waiter grinned.

CHAPTER 11

I was beginning to love Spain and I felt at home there. Granada was as lovely as Father Mike had promised. It was rich in its legacy of Arab architecture and the air was laden with the perfume of flowers and orange blossoms.

One afternoon we visited Alhambra Palace, a fourteenth-century jewel of Moorish architecture, nestled in the red clay hills. One of the most spectacular sights anywhere it is Europe's only medieval palace. The rest of the fortresses and castles were created for defense rather than pleasure. To me the Alhambra Palace was an Arabian Nights fairy tale of fantasy, with its lacy ornamentation and lush gardens. I was touched by the magic of this Andalusian wonder and I was eager to explore.

I said, "Come on, Father Mike, let's go tower-climbing. The guide said we can see all of the city of Granada from the turret."

At this moment an incident occurred which severely shook my confidence in Father Mike and our future. As we crossed the Patio de los Arrayanes, Father Mike suddenly stopped, looked surprised and muttered, "Wait a minute. Wait here." Then he bolted down a path leading away from the palace.

I stood in the middle of the courtyard and watched him disappear. I didn't know what had frightened him or what was happening. I waited for him at the bottom of the tower. I thought, where has he gone? Surely he's coming back. He has the passports and I don't have one peseta and I can't speak a word of Spanish! My mind was racing. Let's see. The name of the hotel was...Oh, my God, what was the name of the hotel? Father Mike, where are you? What in the hell are you doing? This is not a funny game.

Fighting back tears, I looked all over the palace for him. An hour later I was standing at the entrance, shaking, feeling very pregnant and terrified.

Where is he? I wondered. Will I have to go to the American Embassy and have them contact the States and once again be at the mercy of my mother? Will they arrest me for my fake passport? Tears started to fall.

All of a sudden, a speeding cab appeared, the door flew open and I saw Father Mike crouched down in the back seat. He frantically motioned me into the cab. I was dumbfounded. I couldn't move.

"Get in the fucking car!" he called out hoarsely. I seemed to be moving in a dream as I stumbled into the cab.

"Father Mike, where did you go?" I sobbed.

"Never you mind! Do you know who those two women were?"

"What two women?" I said, still shaking.

"That was the Mayor's wife and her friend from Palm Springs walking toward the tower. I should have known better! I forgot they come to Spain every spring. Of all my Irish luck."

"But I don't understand, Father Mike. Sooner or later you will have to face people. We can't keep running and hiding, Father Mike! The truth will come out."

"Yes, I know that, Royal, but not now, not now. I'm not ready yet. It would be all over Palm Springs by the time a wire could cross the Atlantic if they saw us here."

"I'm sure the fact we are together has already gone all over Palm Springs if my mother had anything to do with it. But she can't do anything to you, Father Mike. Bishop Buddy can't do anything to you. You handed in your resignation! What are you afraid of?"

Father Mike looked worn and introspective. "I don't know. You're right about facing the truth, but it's too soon now. I don't want your mother to know where we are. I don't want our whereabouts known in Palm Springs yet."

We rode down the winding hills in silence, separated by our own thoughts. This event had seriously shaken me. I had felt so completely abandoned and vulnerable on that castle hill. Father Mike's impulse to run frightened me. Plagued by dark thoughts, I began to worry about his cowardice. Did he really love me? Did he really intend to marry me? At forty-nine what was he doing with a twenty-one-year-old? Was he really going to become honest about himself and the priesthood? I adored Father Mike and was finally escaping Queen Kong, but what was he doing?

This disturbing event passed without further discussion. But I began to realize how dependent I was on Father Mike. I had closed the door on my old life and its material power and stepped into uncharted territory with Father Mike because I trusted him. My future and my baby's future rested in his hands. There was no safety net underneath me and no turning back. After the incident at Alhambra Palace, I found myself becoming more guarded with him. I took care not to irritate him. We returned to the playful banter that glossed over the rough undercurrents of our individual uncertainties and we continued to connect hungrily in the fires of our sexual passion.

CHAPTER 12

A few days later I awakened to the touch of feathery kisses on my face.

"And a very good mornin' to you, Mrs. O'Donohoe. You look to have slept with the angels, you do."

I stretched contentedly, "Mmm, Father Mike, why are you so sweet and affectionate?"

"Well, darlin', could it be that I love you? And I have quite a treat in store for us tonight."

"You mean the Gypsies?"

"Yes, we'll be goin' up into the Gypsy *cuevas* at Sacro Monte to see them dance."

"What's a *cuevas*?" I asked.

"They are caves. There are hundreds of them and the Gypsies have lived in them for centuries."

"Is this Flamenco dancing?" I asked excitedly.

"The very thing. This is where it comes from, here in Andulusia."

72

"Their caves are their homes and we're allowed to go in and watch them dance there?" I asked.

"The Gypsies are poor and they make money off of the people who come to see their dancing," Father Mike explained.

I spent the day anticipating being inside a Spanish Gypsy's home. When I was eleven, my father's secretary was hired to take me to see the famous dancer, Jose Greco, at the Shubert theater in downtown Chicago. I remembered the frenzied energy of his black shiny boots beating the floor like a woodpecker while his controlled torso moved powerfully in slow motion. I couldn't wait to see the origin of this fiery dance. As we were leaving the hotel Father Mike told me to leave my purse behind.

When I asked him why he said, "Because the Gypsies are known to be thieves."

Our cab wound up the hillside, thickly covered with prickly pear cacti and dotted with caverns. It was dusk when we arrived. We entered the dimly lit "*cueva*," which consisted of several rooms carved out of the hillside and transformed through many generations into crude but cozy living quarters.

The planked wooden floor was painted with a design of black and white geometric squares to create the illusion of tiles. Rough white-washed walls were hung with gleaming copper pots, spoons and ladles, garish religious images and faded family photographs in cheap plastic frames. The air in the small *cueva* was still and heavy with the memory of timeless odors, a fusion of garlic and peppers, dark amber sherry and manzanilla wine, stale cigarette smoke and the sweat of Flamenco.

We were invited to sit down at one of the five small wooden tables that were pushed back against the walls to make room for the dancing. Father Mike ordered Sangrías for us. The remaining tables were filled by a few other uncertain tourists and then by members of the entertainer's family, who positioned themselves around the guitarist and singer. They began to clap their hands joining in the mounting rhythms in a way that was simultaneously passionate, yet casual. The room filled with the running reverberating sounds of the guitar interlaced with the ancient wailing chant of the singer. The moment I had been waiting for arrived. There was silence. The frayed curtain at the back of the *cueva* swept aside and the first dancer entered the room. She walked slowly with pride to the center of the floor where, her back sharply arched, her head held high, she struck a timeless pose, the haughty temptress awaiting her own climactic explosion. She wore a bright pink dress with a plunging bodice that revealed the contours of her sinewy back. Her skirt followed the line of her ample hips, ending at her ankles in tiers of boisterous polka dot ruffles. Soon I was swept away by the petulant rhythms, the relentless staccato beating of her heels, the passion embodied in her controlled movements. There was an ominous concentration of emotion displayed in the scowl on her face and in the taut tendons of her neck. It was as if she were stamping hate, love, birth, death, ageless rebellion and despair into the very earth of Spain. I felt a kinship with her as if I had been drawn into her very shoes.

The intensity of the first dancer was matched and then surpassed by the electric energies of the next couple that began their dance. Slowly, seductively they circled one another, their attraction heightened by the haunting warble of the singer's voice. His torso erect, his head thrown back, bent arm positioned at his back, he displayed his virility with abrupt turns and staccato strikes of his boots. She danced coldness and rejection with haughty flicks of her head, jerks of her shoulders. His dark eyes flashed anger, his body twisted and brooded, his pain mirrored by the singer's cry, a sound beyond words, like an Arab's call to prayer. His pouting persistence mingled with anger. He approached her now with intense desire, heels hammering faster and faster. He encircled her waist and pulled her close, dominating her. The *cueva* was with them, shouting and clapping, encouraging their union, their own passions aroused. Seduced by his violent passion, she allowed her rebellious spirit to be tamed. Their blood boiled. They held each other with their fiery eyes, moving in an ever tightening circle, their bodies in unison, their feet in the same rapid cadence. I followed them to this crescendo. For me, all of Gypsy Spain seemed to be expressing itself in this little room. The dancers had transcended their surroundings and their souls now joined in another reality, where they had been released by the power of Flamenco.

When the dancing ended, we sat transfixed at our table, digesting the journey we had just taken. The doors to the *cueva* were opened and the fragrant night air was allowed to enter the room. We heard the distant barking of dogs and the trailing sound of Flamenco from the neighboring *cuevas*.

A woman with a scrawny infant clinging to her breast stretched out her hand, begging, "*Peseta, peseta por favor.*"

Father Mike brusquely pushed her aside as he steered me toward a waiting cab.

She boldly approached us again and gesturing toward her swollen belly, pathetically pleaded, "*Embarazada, embarazada, peseta, por favor.*"

"Don't ask me for charity, I didn't get you into that condition," Father Mike responded, slamming the door of the cab in her face.

I was shocked by his words and his coldness.

"How could you be so heartless, Father Mike?" I said, as we headed back toward town.

"You have to be, otherwise they'll be all over you. You

should know that, Royal; you've been to India."

"Yes, I understand, but that woman was pregnant."

"Well, what do you expect when all they do is screw," he replied.

I sighed and sunk back into the seat of the cab. "Well, Father Mike, that's all we ever do," I said softly.

I inhaled the heavy perfume of orange blossoms as we wound back down the hill to our hotel. The physical passion of the Gypsy dance still lingered in me. I could feel the throbbing echoes of their staccato rhythms in my body and I hungered for a climax of my own.

Father Mike was aroused too. While carrying on a one-way conversation for the benefit of the cab driver and keeping his gaze straight ahead, he had slipped his hand under my blouse and began slowly caressing my nipples. I squirmed with pleasure under his touch and buried my head in his shoulder to muffle the small, animal sounds of arousal that were rising in my throat.

I groped for him but he pressed my hand onto his thigh whispering, "If you touch me now, I won't be getting out of the cab."

We grabbed the key from the night clerk and ran up the tiled stairs, not waiting for the elevator. We unlocked the door and without turning on the lights, pulled each other down onto the squeaky wood-framed bed. I tore at Father Mike's belt and then at his zipper while he struggled to pull down my skirt, which in the last month had become unbearably tight. We wrestled to free each other's bodies.

"Pull off my panties," I whispered urgently, feeling the heat of his penis on my thigh, wanting him and wriggling to get under him.

"Wrap your legs around me," he breathed huskily.

"Does it still qualify as the missionary position if I do?" I asked, locking my legs around his buttocks and pulling him into me.

This night our lovemaking mirrored the Gypsy dance. With slow and controlled thrusts Father Mike teased me, he held himself back enticing me to join his rhythm. I responded to him, my hips undulating to the beat of the Gyspy music, answering with a rhythm of their own. For a timeless moment we rode the fierce waves of passion in unison, suspended outside of ourselves, attached to this world by a single, slender thread. The fiery explosions of our bodies overlapped as, heads thrown back, we each cried out our own ancient song.

It was a long time before we fell asleep that night. I lay with my head on Father Mike's stomach savoring the mingled odors of our love making. I traced his body with my hand.

"I love your knees, they're so knobby. I hope that our daughter has your knees and not mine."

"I love your whole body, Royal O'Donohoe."

"I love that you're not circumcised, Father Mike Raymond O'Donohoe," I told him as I fondled the malleable folds of his foreskin.

"I'm glad it pleases you, my darlin', since I've been that way since birth," he chuckled.

"No, seriously Father Mike, there is a beauty about it, a naturalness. It's like all the penises I saw in art school."

"Well, circumcision is rarely practiced in Ireland, thank God, or in the rest of Europe for that matter," he said.

"You know, even though you're absolutely sure that our baby is a girl," I said, "I'm glad it will be born in Europe, where, if by the slightest chance it were a boy, he'd be just like you."

CHAPTER 13

I was now almost five months pregnant, and it was time to find a place to settle down. Both Father Mike and I were becoming travel weary, and our finances were getting lean. We needed to establish a home base where Mrs. Sullivan could begin sending Father Mike's monthly income from the Shamrock Daycare Center.

We both wanted to live near the sea. We had heard enthusiastic reports about the colorful southern coast of Spain, known as the Costa del Sol. Near the end of May, we boarded a first-class bus headed for Málaga.

We were situated in our seats, with our luggage stowed overhead, waiting for the bus to leave when Father Mike suddenly jumped up.

"Wait a minute, darlin'. I'll be right back," he said hurriedly, and headed for the front of the bus. I watched him get off and run down the street.

My heart started pounding and my throat became dry. My mind raced. "Who had he seen now who would recognize him? Where was he going?"

I was beginning to hate these "wait" commands.

Once again I faced my vulnerability and my dependence on him. The only words in Spanish I had learned since the terrifying incident at Alhambra Palace were *jamon y queso, por favor* which Father Mike told me I pronounced badly with my American accent.

Just when I was sure the bus would leave without him, Father Mike came flying back with a little cardboard box under his arm.

"You look to have seen a ghost," he said, huffing and puffing and mopping his brow. He settled in next to me just as the bus pulled out.

He placed the box in my lap. "Here's a surprise for you and the little Irish princess," he panted.

Inside the box, on doilies, were delicate flaky Spanish pastries. Like a child whose security has been restored by the reappearance of a loved one bearing a treat, I accepted the box and my fears receded back into the shadows. I didn't say anything to him about how his sudden running off, and how it made me feel.

The bus wound through the red-hued mountains and emerged above the sparkling Mediterranean port of Málaga. We descended through cane fields, through terraced vineyards of Muscatel grapes and hillsides of scarlet strawberries. We used the quiet shady Hotel Miramar in Málaga for a base from which to explore the surrounding towns and villages by bus. On the outskirts of Torremolinos, a little fishing village twelve miles from Málaga, we found a tiny, whitewashed house surrounded by red geraniums on a hill overlooking the glittering blue ocean. Father Mike and I took one look at the uncluttered panorama of fields and sea below, inhaled the fragrance of the sunbaked geraniums and knew we had found our home.

Our house had a bedroom, a kitchen equipped with two hot plates, an abundance of pots and pans, a living room and a red tiled verandah which overlooked the grassy fields and the small fishing settlement below. We had a real, old fashioned ice box.

Twice a week the suave young ice man in his crinkly leather jacket would arrive on his motorcycle to deliver a block of ice, which he transferred into the top of the icebox with a pair of rusty iron tongs. He was always humming one of the latest Top Forty tunes. On Friday morning, old Juan Luis, the stooped, wrinkled, fruit vendor would slowly plod up the hill leading his ancient burro laden with woven baskets filled with oranges, grapes, pears, plums and my very favorite, plump red Bing cherries. I felt like I could sit and eat those cherries until the day I died.

We had a maid named Carmelita who came three times a week to change the linen, wash our clothes and polish the tile floors. Sometimes when her husband had snared rabbits, she brought us a rabbit stew seasoned with local herbs and garlic. I felt so uncomfortable seeing her on her hands and knees laboriously polishing the floors, with large drops of perspiration beading on her forehead, that I told Father Mike I would scrub the floors myself. But he told me her services came with the house and it would be an offense to her to interfere.

Carmelita helped me settle in. I handed her the items out of our suitcases and she carefully folded them and placed them in the chest of drawers, which she had lined with fresh newspaper. Having emptied the bottom of one of Father Mike's suitcases, I casually ran my hand across the upper pocket. I felt the softness of silk and extracted several Countess Mara ties. Then my fingers hit a stiff object in the corner. I pulled it out. It was Father Mike's clerical collar! I stood there transfixed on this object, a symbol of the identity I thought he had left behind. I groped for possible explanations. I could feel my face flush as I noticed Carmelita studying me with wide puzzled eyes. I quickly dropped the collar into the suitcase and slammed the lid shut.

Having been raised by servants, I didn't know much about cooking, but I did my best. I had perfected a wonderful tuna salad, having had to make it for my mother on the maid's day off for years. I was a natural innovator with scrambled eggs after witnessing the concoctions my father cooked up with his imaginary friend, Jim, while drunk. Carmelita showed me how to make ground beef patties with onions and mushrooms. The hardest part was getting the meal from the kitchen to the table without flies landing on it. Spanish flies were hungry and tenacious; they didn't budge when I batted at them. I had to open the kitchen door, carrying food with one hand, shooing flies with the other and run to the table slamming the door behind me before they followed.

Father Mike and I had no extra money for alcohol which was fortunate because it was healthier for all of us, including the baby. I still had had no prenatal care and didn't feel I needed any. I was now wearing my J.C.Penny maternity outfits and feeling proud of my growing belly. In my last month, Father Mike and I would find a doctor in Málaga and make the necessary hospital arrangements.

In Torremolinos our lives became serene and simplified at

last. In the evenings Father Mike and I took our exercise by walking through the fields and down past the fishermen's *casitas* to the sea. I often saw, seated in the doorways and illuminated by candlelight, mothers combing their children's hair for lice. We walked barefoot in the gray sand and stopped to watch the fishermen repairing their webs of salty, reeking nets. The happy sound of children playing nearby mixed with the shrill cry of the gulls overhead. We watched the soft hues of twilight fade and the first stars appear. I made a wish each evening that Father Mike and I would always live in peace like this.

For entertainment we played Scrabble and Father Mike taught me how to play Gin Rummy. After awhile I became so good at it, that when I won, his Irish temper would flair up and he'd throw the cards around the room. We found a tiny, English library in Torremolinos where we checked out books every week. We became avid readers. After a while, I began to relish living away from the glaring chatter of T.V. and radio and I found a deep joy in our simple lifestyle.

One morning, Father Mike and I were in the tub washing each other's hair. He was pouring panfuls of water over my soapy head.

"Would you like to go to Málaga today, Goldilocks, and do our shopping there?" he asked. "We could go to the art supply store and buy some oils and canvases so you can start painting."

"Oh Father Mike, you wonderful, thoughtful man," I said, spitting out soap. I wrapped my swimmer's legs tightly around him. "I'd love that! I've missed my art. I've been thinking of doing a still-life of our checkered tablecloth, some geraniums, and the bounty of fruit that Juan Luis keeps bringing us."

"Well then, paints you shall have. I want you to keep on with your talents," he said, reaching for a towel.

"Do you know the words for the different colors in Spanish?"

I asked, my mind racing over the palette I imagined for my still-life.

Father Mike smiled and said, "You won't have any trouble picking out your colors, Darlin'."

We took the bus to Málaga and filled our baskets with a week's supply of bread, vegetables, eggs, tuna and rice. We also bought soap and the coarse brown toilet paper.

Off the plaza we found an art store where I picked out canvases, brushes, oil paints and a dark wooden palette. When we left the store, I had learned the Spanish words for the primary colors. We had lunch at a sidewalk *tasca* where Father Mike had fried squid and I had a delicious traditional Sopa Malagueña. I was becoming used to the pleading meows of the street cats that were regular customers at the sidewalk cafes. Contented, stuffed and loaded with purchases, we headed to catch the bus to Torremolinos.

"Hurry along," Father Mike urged me, "or we'll miss the bus back."

I was hot and laboring under the weight of my packages.

"Here it comes now," Father Mike said, pulling me along to the bus stop. He leapt onto the crowded bus and turning to me, hollered, "Throw me the canvases and give me your hand. Quick, now!"

I handed him the canvases. and the bus started to move.

"No, let's wait for the next one," I hesitated.

"God damn it, jump up! There won't be another one," he yelled at me.

"No, it's moving too fast. I'm afraid!" I yelled back.

"Jesus, woman...for the love of God, can't you..." he said angrily as the bus pulled away and his voice trailed off.

I stood on the corner and watched him swearing at me from the disappearing bus.

"Here I am," I thought to myself, "five months pregnant and he wants me to jump on a crowded moving bus like an acrobat." I felt exhausted and defeated. "I just can't keep up with him," I thought. I waited on the corner expecting him to return, but after ten minutes had passed, I became frightened that he had gone home without me. Again the familiar pang of abandonment. I was angry at myself for not paying more attention, for always leaving everything up to Father Mike. "Which bus do I take back to Torremolinos?" I began searching frantically in the bottom of my purse for pesetas. Father Mike always carried the money. Father Mike always led the way. Tears of frustration burned on my cheeks.

Then, from across the tree-lined street, I heard Father Mike's voice calling my name. I looked up. There he stood loaded down with baskets and canvases motioning to me. "C'mon, scaredy-cat," he taunted. "Can't you even cross the damned street by yourself?"

His words shot through me like cold steel. Why was he picking on me like this? This was more than just his Irish temper. I lowered my head and fighting back the tears, crossed the busy street.

"What's the matter with you, Royal? Why did you just stand there lollygagging like a stone? You act like such an infant at times. I don't know how the hell you made it around the world with your mother, if you can't even jump on a bus."

I felt a wounded anger explode in my chest.

"The last moving vehicle I tried to jump on, Father Mike, was the Rock Island Line train and I ended up on my face on the side of the tracks. And I never rode on buses with my mother. We went around the world first-class. We had private cars with drivers. You forget, Father Mike, I'm not used to this. I was never <u>allowed</u> to take the bus!"

"Well now, that's a world you've left behind, isn't it?" he snapped.

"I agreed to give up my world for you, but I need some time to adjust, Father Mike. You seem to forget that I'm twenty-seven years younger than you, that I'm pregnant, and that I'm doing the best I can in a strange country."

"Well, all I ask is that you wake up and pay attention to what you're doing, like getting on the bus," he said impatiently.

"What's the difference, Father Mike, whether I got on the damned bus or not," I said, exasperated. "I didn't want to take a chance with the baby."

Father Mike made no reply. We waited for the next bus in silence.

* * *

I began to paint and Father Mike loved my work. He thought I had enormous talent and would often drag Carmelita over by the arm to view my latest canvas. I drew from my painting a deep satisfaction, and free from the proscriptions of art professors, I began to find my own vision and create my own style. After a dozen or so still-lifes, I began to focus on the landscapes around me, working on the verandah in the coolness of the late afternoons to capture the elongated shadows and soft melting light of the end of day.

CHAPTER 14

Father Mike continued to go to mass on Sundays in Torremolinos and at his request I accompanied him. One Sunday morning in late June, after a feast of my variety #37 scrambled eggs, I was mesmerized by the sun glinting on the Mediterranean below, and couldn't face the charade of trooping off to church. I wanted to stay home and paint.

"Father Mike, I'm not going to mass with you this morning," I said.

"Why not?"

"Because it is so crowded and I can't follow it," I hedged.

"Sometimes I think you're a bloody heathen, Royal. The main thing in church is that you are there to honor God, not follow the liturgy exactly."

"I know, but I can't understand why you have to go to church each Sunday. God is everywhere all the time, omnipresent. Surely you don't believe if you miss mass you are going to hell. How can you leave the priesthood and live in sin with a pregnant woman and not think you are already going to hell for that? It doesn't make sense."

"I believe in what I believe and I told you before we left the states that I would continue to be a Catholic and that Dierdre would be raised as one."

"That's fine. It's all right with me, Father Mike, that you go to church and practice your faith, but are you going out of fear as a wayward priest or are you going as an honest man asking for God's help?"

Father Mike's face grew taut. "I am going as a man who has spent his whole life as a priest. I was raised in Ireland to become a priest and I will not abandon my faith whether I am a priest or not."

"I don't want you to abandon your faith, Father Mike, I just want you to examine the fears that are woven into your faith. You have so many superstitions."

"Superstitions? What kind of brainless babbling is that? You are indeed a bloody heathen!" he said, his face reddening.

"Father Mike, you do have superstitions, like thinking that if you use the same water for tea that you boiled eggs in, you'll get warts! I mean, really, Father Mike. You're an intelligent man."

"What in God's name does that have to do with anything?" he shouted.

"It has everything to do with who you are. I just want you to really examine the things you have always believed." I trembled inside knowing I was nearing a nerve. I had never spoken to Father Mike like this before. "I just want you to look at what you're doing, Father Mike. I want you to see the truth. I want us to live in truth. We're still living a lie. We aren't married as you promised we would be, and you run like a rabbit from the people you know." I was looking straight into his eyes, but in my heart I was cringing.

"You brainless girl, the reason I run 'like a rabbit' as you say, is because of your bitch of a mother and her power to make trouble for us. I think you're naive, Royal. You don't realize the ramifications of our situation. I'm the one who has to protect and support us. It's up to me to decide our course."

"What course have you decided on that you're going to need your collar?"

"What are you talking about?"

"I found your collar in your suitcase when Carmelita and I were unpacking. Father Mike, that's the world you left behind, isn't it?"

Father Mike paused. "This may be hard for you to understand, my dear one," he said, subdued, "but if I ever have to return to Ireland, if someone in my family dies, I could never go before them without that collar."

Our conversation ended there and Father Mike went to church. I set up my easel on the verandah, but I didn't feel like painting. I took a bath instead and lay down naked on the bed with a big bowl of cherries and Hemmingway's The Old Man and the Sea, but I couldn't concentrate. I was shaken by my boldness in challenging Father Mike and I worried over what the repercussions might be. I felt I had spoken the truth but feared I had stepped out of bounds with him. I desperately longed for us to be married but I was afraid to push the subject further. It occurred to me that perhaps I should cultivate more patience with Father Mike. I knew I was having difficulty adjusting to my new world; wouldn't it be even harder for him leaving a lifelong vocation behind? I felt compassion for him. I gazed out the window at the calm sea and reflected on how peaceful it all was. I felt grateful to be there. Idly, I placed cherries from the white porcelain bowl into a design on Father Mike's pillow. The cherries spelled out "I LOVE

YOU." Then I must have fallen asleep.

I awoke to familiar feathery kisses and the rich scent of roses. Father Mike had stretched out next to me and a small bouquet of roses lay on my breast. I smiled at him and through drowsy eyes watched him reach over and rearrange the cherries into a new message: "I'M SORRY." I snuggled into his arms.

"I'm sorry too, my darling Father Mike. You are everything to me."

He stroked me softly. "I love to watch you sleep. You sleep like an angel, you do. And I love to feel Dierdre moving about in there," he said, running his hand over the mound of my stomach and then planting tender kisses on my navel.

"She knows you love her and that you've brought us roses," I said, taking his head in my hands and kissing his eyes. I rolled my leg over Father Mike's stomach and positioned myself on top of him. Then I leaned over and dropped a cherry into his mouth. As he chewed it I kissed his mouth hungrily. I felt him swell beneath me.

"You don't think our lovemaking hurts the baby, do you?" he asked tenderly stroking my buttocks.

"In our little medical book it says sex is okay as long as the pregnancy is normal. Remember the diagram? The baby is protected in a bag of water. Besides, this is natural," I said, slowly rocking my hips and licking the cherry juice off his mouth.

"You're the horniest woman I know," he whispered as he slipped inside of me.

"Isn't this the way God intended us to be?"

* * *

90

Father Mike and I shelved the subject of religion. He continued to go to Mass on Sunday mornings, while I continued to stay home and paint on the verandah. I reveled in my pregnancy and felt a sense of completeness now that my life-long dream of being a mother was coming true. Even though the issue of our marriage remained unsettled, Father Mike and I experienced a closeness that neither one of us had known before. He brought me back seashells and odd-shaped rocks from his walks on the beach and I picked wild lavender from the hillsides to sweeten our baths. I blossomed under this closeness and relished these days filled with so much affection.

When we first settled into our house in Torremolinos, Father Mike had advised Mrs. Sullivan of our whereabouts and made arrangements for her to begin sending us his money from the Shamrock Daycare Center along with Harold White's monthly payments. In addition, he instructed her to have Harold forward the trunk that I had so carefully prepared for my new life. I think Father Mike was particularly impatient for me to get my Betty Crocker Cookbook. I couldn't wait to see again the little blankets I had knitted in the Chi Omega house and the baby clothes I had bought in Albuquerque.

CHAPTER 15

When I saw Father Mike's face as he stepped onto the verandah, I knew something was terribly wrong. He had just come back from a trip to Malaga to do the shopping and check for mail. His round Irish face was gray and pinched.

"What's happened?"

"Will you be letting me sit down first?" he said, setting the baskets on the table and dropping into a chair. He pulled a letter out of his pocket. "I've heard from Mrs. Sullivan and things aren't good. She hasn't gotten any money from Harold and hasn't been able to get in touch with him. Apparently he has gone away on a long trip. The luck of the Irish."

"But they have all our things stored at their house and they helped us get away. I don't understand why he wouldn't send you the money he knew we were counting on."

"I never thought he'd pull something like this on me," Father Mike said, shaking his head.

"Do you have it in writing?"

"What in writing?"

"The agreement. You got a statement that you loaned him $10,000, didn't you?"

"No, like a fool I didn't. I did it in friendship and also because I knew he would inherit a chunk when his father died."

"So what are you going to do?"

"There's nothing I can do from here."

"Well, what about the daycare center?"

"Here," he said, thrusting the letter into my hand, "You can read all about the Shamrock Daycare Center."

Mrs. Sullivan's letter failed to hide the distress she felt having to impart bad news to the priest she had been so devoted to for years.

"...Mrs. Phillips has raised a considerable disturbance since your departure. In addition to contacting the Mayor and other of your acquaintances, she frequently calls the Bishop when she is inebriated and makes outlandish accusations. She insists you have spirited her daughter away and sold her into white slavery. Although this sounds incredible, please believe that I am not exaggerating. On June 2, Bishop Buddy sent representatives to Palm Springs to dissolve the Shamrock Daycare Center. They required me to turn over all of your books and files. Please forgive me. I'm so sorry, Father Mike, but I had no choice. The Church lawyers said the Shamrock Daycare Center legally belongs to the Church. My hands were tied.

Mrs. Phillips told Father Arnoldi, who has now permanently replaced you, that she has hired private detectives to find her daughter. She has also contacted the FBI and told them Miss Phillips disappeared out of the country with a priest and that she is under age. It is common knowledge now that when she is drunk Mrs. Phillips loses control of herself and will call anyone at any time and becomes verbally abusive. You should be warned that she is convinced you have kidnapped her daughter and she is out to destroy you. It pains me to bring you this bad news.

Of course I will continue trying to reach Mr. White in Redlands. Meanwhile, please be careful. I am concerned for your welfare. My prayers are with you.

I remain faithfully yours,

Elinor Sullivan.

As I read Mrs. Sullivan's words, I could feel the blood draining from my head and needed to sit down. I recognized the old theme in my mother's actions. In her eyes, I was never worth anything; no one would love me for myself. No one with good intentions would be attracted to me. She thought Father Mike couldn't possibly love me. He had to be using me in some way.

I put down the letter and looked at Father Mike. I felt like the bottom was falling out of my stomach. I nearly fainted. Father Mike mopped his brow.

"What does this all mean, Father Mike?"

"It means that now there will be no money. It means the financial plans I have made for us have gone awry. I know it was your mother's harassment that brought an investigation of the Daycare Center. I know it!" he said, pounding his fist on the chair.

"Well, what will we do now, Father Mike? What can we do?"

"We will have to return to the States, my darlin', for I can't see how we can continue to live here with no income. We are running low on money as it is now."

"Father Mike, this can't be happening," I said, turning toward the sea and the horizon which I had grown to love.

In the days that followed we had many discussions about where to go, about where it would be safe to go.

"Once we're back in the States, I can track Harold down,"

Father Mike said. "And I can have a go at all the others who owe me favors, and there are plenty of them. I should be able to come up with something. After all I wasn't the priest to all those movie stars for nothing."

* * *

We decided to go to Phoenix. Father Mike knew the area and his contacts were nearby. He felt my mother would be unlikely to track us to a city practically under her nose. I remembered Phoenix from my love trysts with Father Mike when I was at the university and I had a good feeling about it.

Carmelita helped us pack. She brought us one of her famous rabbit stews for our farewell dinner. She sensed my sadness at leaving and embraced me warmly, wrapping her brown arms around my bulging stomach and whispering something in Spanish to the baby.

To save money, Father Mike decided we would sail back to America. He booked third-class passage for us on a large Italian ship called the Michelangelo, which would take us from Gibraltar to New York. Early on the morning of July sixth, we stood on the main road behind our house waiting for the country bus from Málaga that would take us to Gibraltar. The morning sun was already hot. Father Mike was in an optimistic mood as he organized our pile of suitcases, my bundle of art supplies, and my paintings that we had wrapped carefully with brown corrugated paper and string.

"This will be an adventure, riding the local bus along the Costa del Sol, and then, my dearie darlin', when we get to Gibraltar, we'll have a proper tea time, British style," he said, making an attempt to keep my spirits lifted.

I heard the drone of the approaching bus laboring up the hill. Father Mike flagged it down and struggled to hand our luggage up to the driver who added it to the heap of boxes and suitcases already roped onto the roof of the bus. Then he took my arm and escorted me aboard. The bus was packed with farmers toting boxes and baskets of local produce, old men with deep, sunbaked lines creasing their faces, women with nursing babies and rowdy pubescent boys punching and poking at each other. Father Mike and I pushed our way back to the last two empty seats. At the next town, a dozen or so people stood on the side of the road waiting for the bus. I thought surely we wouldn't stop as there was no more room, but that was my American idea of space. Several men elected to climb onto the top of the bus and ride with the luggage while the rest of the passengers squeezed into the aisles. Father Mike gallantly offered his seat to an elderly señora who wrestled with a pair of large straw baskets containing live chickens. She eased her portly body down next to me and settled the baskets of chickens on the floor between us. I instantly found that my fear of animals definitely included poultry. I was terrified by the beady-eyed chicken that craned its neck out of the basket and made random pecking motions in the vicinity of my skirt. I had never looked at a chicken up close. I watched it while frozen in a state of captivated revulsion and speculated on the morbid end that awaited it. My heart rate returned to normal when a few stops later, the chicken lady disembarked and was replaced by a young woman, who sat down, unbuttoned her blouse and began to nurse her baby. I had seen this all over Spain, women nursing their babies in public. I thought about America and how uncommon breast feeding was there. And the rare woman who did nurse her baby, did so modestly behind closed doors. I thought the Spanish way was natural, and I decided then and there that I would nurse my baby.

After leaving the bus we had to show our passports at La Linea, the last point in Spain.

"Father Mike, what about my new passport?" I asked as we approached the guards.

"Just hold your head up high and act cool."

"But what if my mother's detectives have gotten this far?"

"I doubt it, Royal. We'll say a prayer. It'll be all right, you'll see." He squeezed my hand.

"Say a prayer? You say the prayer." I could feel my heart beating faster as we stood in line waiting for our turn.

The immigration official grabbed my passport and peered at my face over his glasses. I held my breath and smiled. He brusquely stamped the paper. I stood to the side waiting for Father Mike to get processed. We got a taxi to drive us across the narrow airport runway, which serves as the entrance to the British territory of Gibraltar.

I said, "I almost passed out back there. I hate this feeling, like we're criminals being hunted."

"We are criminals being hunted but you did great. I'm proud of you."

Gibraltar is a bustling town on a rock that is just four miles long and half a mile wide. During the three days that Father Mike and I waited for the Michelangelo to depart we tried to forget about our uncertain future by just being tourists. We encountered the mischievous, cinnamon-colored, tail less Barbary apes in their den on Old Queens Road. The British believe that as long as the apes remain on Gibraltar, the Rock will be British. There is a special post in the British Army, "Officer of the Apes," whose sole job is to feed them twice a day.

We took a train to the top of the Rock, which offers a panoramic view of the straits between Spain and Morocco. In a restaurant, which seemed to overlook the world, I summoned the courage to bring up the subject of marriage again. I was afraid to ask why we hadn't gotten married in Spain as Father Mike had promised. I suspected it was because a wedding in Spain meant getting married in the Catholic Church. Maybe he believed he would burn in a special hell for that. Father Mike ordered lamb stew for himself and prime rib for me. We each had an English ale. We made a toast to each other and to the next chapter in our uncertain life. When I asked Father Mike if he was going to marry me when we returned to the States, he took the question in stride.

"Of course I am, darlin'," he replied. "Dierdre can't grow up with us not married. Her road will be hard enough as it is. For that matter, all our roads will be hell until your mother is off my neck and accepts our situation. I am going to try to get in touch with Harold as soon as we get to Phoenix and there are a couple of people, who, I am almost certain, will loan me money. Once we get that straightened out, we can plan a little ceremony. Christine could fly over and be your maid of honor. That would please you, wouldn't it, my angel," he said, beaming his irresistible charm at me.

* * *

The Michelangelo was the newest ship on the Italia line and she was splendid. Third-class swarmed with Italian peasants making their way to America for the first time. There were only two other American couples besides us in this sea of black-clad immigrants. Each night an assortment of enthusiastic Italians gathered around the cramped corner bar and made their own lively entertainment. A boisterous jovial music sprang from their crude concertinas and loud raucous voices, often drawing first-class passengers down from the staid ballroom where they grew tired of sitting stiffly in starched tuxedos politely listening to chamber music.

On these occasions, Father Mike and I were often the center of attention. He took the stage instinctively, charming the English-speaking passengers with stories and anecdotes told in a lilting brogue. We were also the darlings of the crew because we were among the few third-class passengers who tipped.

Unaccustomed to travel and their equilibrium upset by the ships roll, the Italian peasants heaved vomit on their black clothes and beyond. We had to watch where we stepped at all times. I wondered how they managed to clean their one and only set of clothes. Once again, I never got seasick.

In New York harbor, Father Mike and I tightly gripped each other's hand as we descended the gangplank of the Michelangelo and approached the immigration counters. I was praying to God that there would be no surprise welcoming committee from the FBI, and that our names would not be on some wanted list. We were surrounded on all sides by our third-class Italian companions in their dark crumpled clothes, full of fear and wonderment. We loomed above them in both physical and social stature, Father Mike in his tailor-made suit and Countess Mara tie, I with my blond hair and floral maternity dress. We inched our way forward, Father Mike mopping his brow. We both shifted uneasily as we presented our passports at the immigration desk at the entrance to the large concrete terminal.

"I see this passport was issued in Seville," the immigration official said, peering at me over the top of his glasses.

"Yes, that's because my old passport expired while I was there," I offered.

After a few more routine questions he stamped our passports and then said to us, "Would you step to the side over here please and wait." He motioned us toward an area next to the luggage bin.

"What for?" I asked, my heart racing.

"For a customs check," he said with a cool briskness, turning to signal two uniformed customs officials to come forward.

"Oh, Jesus Christ," I heard Father Mike utter under his breath.

Our luggage was identified and placed on a metal table. The strings on my paintings were cut and the brown paper removed. We were asked to unlock our suitcases. What were they looking for? Did we look like smugglers? I watched as they rifled through every inch of our belongings. My breath caught in my throat when I saw Father Mike's clerical collar pass through their hands as they sifted through his clothing. Father Mike had turned white as a ghost.

An hour and a half after setting foot on American soil, our suitcases were slammed shut, the wrapping on my paintings was taped back together, customs seals were placed on our luggage and we were admitted into the country.

"What was that all about, Father Mike? What were they looking for?" I asked as we hurriedly followed the porter who pushed our baggage toward a taxi stand in front of the harbor terminal.

"I don't know. I have no idea. Let's just get out of here," Father Mike snapped, cramming the bags into the taxi and herding me into the back seat.

Father Mike and I spent three days in New York City and every time I saw a policeman, fear struck.

CHAPTER 16

We were greeted by a blast of 107-degree heat when we landed Phoenix. We had only enough money to rent a car for one day, during which time we found a studio apartment on West Glenrosa and furnished it with the bare essentials. It could soar up to 120 degrees in summertime Phoenix. The saving grace of our flat-roofed sterile apartment was the fact that it had air-conditioning and a swimming pool in the center courtyard. A few aluminum lounge chairs were scattered around on the painted green concrete, bordering the pool. Down at the end facing the units was a picnic area with a red metal Coke machine and a fake adobe barbecue pit.

There was still no word or money from Harold White. We were existing on practically nothing. We had one set of sheets, our Scrabble board, and a library card in a fictitious name. That was it.

I learned to make chicken livers and all kinds of strange things that didn't cost much. I asked the butcher for treats for my non-existent cat and used the chicken necks he gave me for soup.

Things grew tense. Wedding plans were never discussed.

Father Mike found a Catholic obstetrician and took me to him for prenatal care. He had a private conference with the doctor while I waited in the reception room. On the way home on the bus, I found out that he had told the doctor that he was a Catholic priest and that he had gotten me pregnant and that he had no money. He had asked the doctor to please take me on as a confidential charity case. I was horrified. I realized how much I had left behind to go off with this man. My family had disowned me and I was now a charity case. Reduced to the ranks of the needy. I had slid from the best of everything, to the bottom. Now that Father Mike was pretending to be a priest again, if he was pretending, I saw no immediate marriage in sight for us. I faced having an illegitimate child and becoming an unwed mother.

Since I was a small child, I had felt apart from the life around me, a visitor in my parents' house, a spectator to their dramas, but now this drama of my own that I had dared to embrace had led me to become an outcast of society. I felt helpless and demoralized. How could Father Mike let this happen to us, to me? I had so willingly put my life in his hands, so blithely trusted that he could provide for us. I knew that there was no turning back because I loved Father Mike, so I followed the only course that was open to me. I did what I had always done. I put one foot in front of the other. I suppressed my shame and swallowed my resentment. I turned my focus to the miracle of life inside me and I turned to God as I perceived Him, fervently asking for His protection. I prayed to Him to help Father Mike to find a way to turn our situation around.

CHAPTER 17

The thing that kept me sane at this time was swimming. I swam back and forth. I had gone to J.C. Penney and purchased one pink maternity bathing suit and I swam until the thing fell apart. The neighbors teased me that our baby would be a mermaid. The 100-degree heat drove Father Mike into the pool with me and after a while he had no other recourse than to submit to my swimming lessons. These usually took place at twilight when the rest of the residents had gone inside to dinner.

"You're daft if you think I'm going to flounder around in front of all the neighbors," Father Mike had told me. "Its bad enough having you cradling me around in the water like a wee baby."

My technique was to first teach him to float and I did this by having him lie on his back while supporting his body, one hand under his head, the other under his buttocks.

"C'mon now, you have to let go and trust me," I coaxed him. "Just relax. Lie back on the water, I've got you. Remember, the water is your friend."

We went through this routine over and over. I sometimes had the urge to giggle seeing Father Mike in such a vulnerable position. Humorous pictures would pop into my mind of what would happen if I let go of him. I could see him caving in at the middle, flopping and spluttering like an awkward duck, spewing Irish profanities. But I never let go and finally one evening he allowed himself to float and we moved onto the crawl.

By late July I was in my eighth month of pregnancy and we were counting every penny. I was learning to do wild things with food. I made casseroles with potato skins. After we made morning tea, I saved all the tea bags and on weekends, boiled them again for iced tea. To save bus fare, Father Mike taught me how we would hitchhike. It was 1961, and I had never heard of a woman hitchhiking. We would walk to Indian School Road where we would wait in the 107-degree sun while he flagged down a car. He would ask if they were going downtown, and could they give him and his pregnant wife a lift to her doctor's appointment. This would be our mode of transportation until the day of my labor. Standing on the side of the road, waiting for rides in the scorching heat, I often thought of our dependable chauffeur Vinson, and how embarrassing it was to me to be driven in the rear seat of a Cadillac. My mind drifted back to when I was six years old in Chicago, holding Vinson's strong black hand as he safely delivered me each morning to the black hooded Sisters of Mercy at Academy of Our Lady.

On the way to my check-up one afternoon in mid-August, Father Mike and I waited for a ride for twenty minutes, sweating in the merciless sun until a middle-aged Indian couple in a dusty old Plymouth finally stopped to pick us up. I leaned my head on Father Mike's shoulder and dozed on and off, half listening to the static Country Western music droning from the car radio. My reverie was broken by a deep baritone voice delivering the hourly news. I whispered into Father Mike's ear, "In New Mexico, most of the people I knew hated the Indians. Look at how kind they are to give us a ride."

"There is always the underdog no matter where you live. But we are all children of God."

"My child is truly a child of God, isn't she, Father Mike?"

The only person I was in contact with was my trustworthy sorority sister, Christine, with whom I had shared the truth of this journey from the beginning. She remained loyal and silent. Her letters to me in Phoenix were my only contact with the outside world. I would go to my mailbox hungry for the world her letters brought to me. I was often depressed. Being on the lam is like that. There is a loneliness that begins to gnaw at you when you are in forced isolation. Sometimes Father Mike would write surprise letters and put them in the mailbox for me to find. He would write that he knew this was hard for me, but that together we would get through it. His letters were magnificent, eloquent, and they fed my spirit for a while.

> My Dearie Darlin',
> I watch you sleep at night and
> know the angels are dancin'
> around your beautiful face.
> My arm encircled around you, I
> feel Dierdre moving about
> beneath your skin. I know she
> is as healthy as her mother.
> It won't be long now until you
> will have a tiny mermaid to
> swim by your side. I want you
> to put all thoughts of your
> mother's fracas behind you. I
> loathe seeing you go through
> this and know that at times,
> you must get lonely. I admire
> your courage. I think you
> know we are in love now more
> than ever. Soon we will not
> be policed. We will be safe
> and I will be free.
> Love,
> Your Mike

CHAPTER 18

Father Mike continued to receive communication from Mrs. Sullivan, repeating that his original plan for our support had fallen apart, and that my mother continued her drunken rages, threatening revenge and accelerating the search for us. Whenever I suggested that surely he could do something about our situation by getting a job, he would get angry.

"People don't just hire a priest, Royal. What am I going to do, put twenty-five years of hearing confessions and saying mass on a résumé? That would surely give people a good laugh."

"But somebody out there would certainly hire a priest, Father Mike."

I thought of all his education, of his charisma, his instinctive showmanship, his ability to lead and inspire people. Couldn't he see his own potential? Was it shame keeping him from transferring his skills as a priest into a job that would save us?

"Father Mike, you have so many talents," I told him. "You could do anything."

"I've gone that route before, Royal, many times. The last time I left the priesthood, I let someone lend me a hand and talk me into selling ice-cream contracts. The fellow said I would make a killing with all my persuasive social talents. Talents be damned. I could barely eke out a living for myself."

"Well, you could be a bartender, anything, it doesn't have to be permanent, just a job until you find Harold or you think of something else."

"Don't press me on this, Royal," he said authoritatively. "You're lucky to have me with you. I haven't let you down. I've stood by you. You could have ended up in one of those homes like girls do."

My eyes widened.

"I could put you into an unwed mothers' home, like a Florence Crittenden place. I don't have to stay with you, you know," he said. "The unwed mothers' home is around the corner."

This threat of betrayal that he would leave me in an unwed mothers' home hit me like a thunderbolt. His words stabbed my ears. The threat hung in the air like icy needles. There it was: the threat of abandonment. The old pain from my childhood awakened, slithered into the present. Father Mike was the father. My father had abandoned me by traveling and leaving me with a drunken mother and then by dying. Now here was my lover, the priest, the ultimate all-time father threatening to abandon me. I thought of the times I had awakened in the night and watched Father Mike's chest rise and fall with his breathing. In those moments the fear always lurked in me that his heart would stop as my father's had and I would be left alone again.

I had left everything behind, all connections to family and friends, my very identity. I trusted him. I had handed him my power, and now my future and my baby's future rested in his hands.

I felt the rage well up in me. I screamed at him, "Father Mike, in the very beginning I offered to have an abortion so none of this would have happened. It was you who wanted us to keep our child. You even named her! We left the country so we could have her and a life together. We love each other. How could you threaten me with something like this? That's something my mother would do. How could you entertain such an idea? What has happened to you?"

"What has happened, my little Miss Pollyanna, is that I didn't know then that Harold would weasel out of paying on his loan or how much trouble your mother would cause. Don't you realize now that your mother will haunt us 'til the day we die, making trouble and ruining our lives and the child's reputation? We will never have a moment's rest."

"But you knew from the beginning that my mother was a complete bitch, a maniac."

"But I didn't know to what lengths she would go. I didn't know she would be bringing the Church down on my Shamrock Daycare Center. That was our income, Royal, that and the money from Harold. We're broke. Our backs are against the wall."

"Then what are we going to do? What does that mean, Father Mike?"

"Don't you see, Royal, it means we can't keep this child. It's just not going to work."

The words slowly penetrated my body. An iron fist seized my stomach and I felt my legs begin to buckle. The heaviness in my womb grew unbearable. I reached for the nearest chair and slumped down.

"We'll get married and we'll have more children later, but we can't keep this child," I heard Father Mike say from the end of a narrowing tunnel.

"We can't keep this child?" I repeated weakly. "We can't keep this child? We'll get married, married later and have another child?

My God, Father Mike, what are you saying, what's happening?"

"Look at us, Royal. We're practically living on cat food. Do you think we can raise a baby like this? Do you think it makes me proud to have you be a charity case?"

"Father Mike, then I will go to work. Let me work. I'll do anything to keep us together," I said, in tears, sliding to my knees in front of his chair and tightly circling my arms around his waist.

"You can't work now," he said, his blue eyes fastening onto mine. "You're almost ready to give birth. Think about the kind of life this child would have. There is no chance for her to have a normal one, or for us either, with no money and your mother sworn to sabotage us. We're going to have to put this baby up for adoption."

The world receded for me behind a curtain of tears. I retreated into myself. I thought, this can't be. I'm moving in a dream. This just can't be.

* * *

As the broiling days of August passed, I kept believing that some miracle was going to take place, that our baby would be saved and we would go on as a family. Every night I prayed that somehow this miracle would occur. Every night I tossed and turned with nightmares. I would awaken and gently massage my swollen stomach and softly talk to my baby.

"Dierdre, everything will be all right. I know that we'll all stay together."

I could feel her kicking and moving about inside of me as if she were truly listening.

"There, there, sweet baby. I love you so much. Calm down and let mommy sleep."

Father Mike would often wake up and ask, "Who are you talking to?"

"I'm talking to Dierdre, of course."

"Sometimes I think you are a bit daft, Royal. Let's get some sleep."

But the sleep would not come. There were many nights when I would think about my options. I had none. I was trapped. He was older and was supposed to have all the answers. To avoid being abandoned, I succumbed.

* * *

Just a few weeks before the baby was due, Father Mike flagged down a car and took me to the Catholic Social Services to arrange the adoption interview. I was treated like a number. I was treated as if this momentous act of giving up a child were no more than a casual public transaction. It was as if I were buying a bus ticket.

No one spoke to me in a friendly voice. No one treated me as if I mattered. I was simply a vehicle for a soon-to-be-adopted Catholic baby. I had wanted to be a mother since I was seven years old, and now I was looking at the prospect of giving this precious child over as a gift to the world. How could this act be treated so coldly and without honor?

On the day of the interview, I sat in a gray cubicle on a metal chair and answered the questions the thin-lipped social worker asked of me while avoiding my eyes and shifting uneasily in her chair. Apparently she was uncomfortable around sinners.

Agitated by her coldness I mustered up my courage. "Look Miss," I said, "this is a very special baby coming here. I didn't get knocked up in the back of a pickup truck after the prom. This is the baby of a very intelligent Catholic priest." I hoped this would count for something in the Catholic adoption point system. "You know, the gene pool is good here," I continued. "We wanted this baby. She was made out of love."

I waited for a sign that she had comprehended my communication but there was no response, save a mechanical, "uh huh," and the continuous shuffling of papers.

I stopped pleading and questioning Father Mike. I was afraid of his anger and what he might do if I badgered him. I fiercely, desperately hung on to the idea that some miracle would happen and I would be able to keep our baby. I knew the adoption would not be final until after the birth, when I would have to sign the last papers.

One blistering afternoon when my spirits had fallen into the basement of depression, Father Mike put his arms around me and suggested I go look in the mailbox. I was always anxious to get news from Christine but when I looked in the box I recognized Father Mike's handwriting on an envelope crudely decorated with hearts. I took the letter out to the pool and under the shade of the green plastic corrugated roof of the picnic area, I sat and read.

"My dearie darlin' Royal,

This is a sad time for us, requiring a difficult but nonetheless inevitable decision. We must take an action we both loathe. I want you to know that I have loved you from the very moment I laid eyes on you, and I have never stopped. You are my angel. We will come through this together. I ask for your patience to give me time to turn my life around and onto the path we once envisioned, and then there will be more children, children we can raise in a safe and sane environment. I am counting on you to be strong. Trust me as I know what's best for you. You are the very beating of my heart, my love.

Your Mike.

CHAPTER 19

My water broke at dawn. I heard it. There was a dull popping sound and then I felt warm liquid oozing between my legs. I lay there for a few minutes feeling this strange phenomenon, before I woke up Father Mike.

"Father Mike, I think something's happening to my body," I whispered.

"Do you think the baby's coming now?"

"Yeah. I'm having small rhythmic cramps and I think my bag of waters popped--there's liquid coming out of me."

I went to the bathroom and I sat on the toilet. There was a blood-tinged mucous coming out of me and I remembered the medical travel book calling this "the bloody show."

"Now I have some blood!" I called to Father Mike.

"I'd best get dressed and go down to the manager's apartment to call the doctor then," he said, his voice sounded concerned.

"While you're there, do you think you could ask him if he would give us a ride to the hospital?"

Father Mike was rushing around nervously, brushing his teeth, and looking for something to wear. He pulled on a pair of Bermuda shorts and grabbed a shirt.

I called to him from the bed.

"Wait awhile please. Come over here and just hold me. Hold me tight, Father Mike. I'm a little frightened."

"There, there, Royal," he said, patting me while I nuzzled my head against his chest. "Women have babies every day. You're going to be just fine."

I could hear his heart thumping rapidly underneath his black shirt.

Coming to childbirth with little knowledge and so few ideas of what to expect made my experience a raw one, unshaped by preconceived ideas, beauty-parlor patter, or old wives' tales. This was the time when even under the best of circumstances you didn't ask questions of your doctor. He was the boss. You put yourself into his hands and trusted. The doctor said, "Don't worry, I'll take care of everything."

I was introduced to birth from within. As early as a few days before the birth, I had begun to be guided by my instincts. I had known exactly when to stop swimming. Childbirth began in a gentle manner, like a stream moving through me. Then it picked up speed and began to widen into a river. It was a force over which I had no control. I simply went with it. I knew instinctively when it was time to go to the hospital and I asked Father Mike to tell the manager I was ready.

* * *

The Arizona sun has no mercy, even in mid-morning. The manager's car had no air-conditioning and with each passing pain I struggled to breath. "I really thank you...Senor Garcia...This ride means a lot to me," I said.

"Think nothing of it Mrs. O'Donohoe. It's not every day I get to deliver precious cargo." He smiled and winked at me. "Don't worry about a thing. I'm the last of thirteen children, and my mother, *gracias a Dios*, never had a problem."

Father Mike blurted out, "She's not going to have any problems." With one of his hands, he grabbed my arm. I could feel beads of sweat on his hand. With his other hand, he mopped his brow.

He repeatedly tried to reassure me about the future. He whispered, "Royal, everything's going to be all right. Believe me, everything will be all right. I'm going to take care of you. I think we'll go to San Diego after this. I know some people there who can help us to start over."

I smiled at him and in my mind refused to accept any part of it. I was still determined some miracle would occur and I would keep the baby.

"Believe me when I say we will have a life together," he continued.

* * *

In the early 1960s, St. Joseph's Hospital, off Central Avenue in downtown Phoenix was very progressive. The fathers were allowed to stay with the mothers in the labor room. It was my good fortune to have a bed by a window.

Father Mike stayed with me during the first part of my labor, which lasted all day. The contractions came and went one after the other, but I was able to talk with him and play some gin rummy. By afternoon I was starving and begged Father Mike to smuggle me in something to eat. He came back with four oily cookies in his pocket, and one flower. One pink carnation. I stared at that carnation. I picked it up and smelled its spicy sweetness.

He said, "With your next baby, you'll have a room full of flowers."

Tears welled in my eyes and I thought, "And they will never mean as much as this one."

I was dozing in and out. I would open my eyes and see Father Mike silhouetted against the window, in the familiar pose of mopping his brow. Behind him, the sky was ablaze with streaks of orange and pink, the desert paintbrush at work.

As the pains of labor increased, I let them wash over me. The contractions seemed to engulf my being. I felt vulnerable and afraid as my body opened wider and wider, a sensation beyond my control. And deep within me, a song of jubilation rose over the screeching pain, fatigue, and fear: I was fulfilling my lifetime desire to give birth.

I awoke abruptly to big, intense, jagged contractions. There was no holding back, now. The river had swollen into a tidal wave. My body felt as if it were turning inside out. When I needed help, I was supposed to ring the buzzer above the bed. I looked at the buzzer, and I knew that I had to ring it. Yet it was so hard for me to do so. I had been raised by my mother never to call for help or to ask for anything. We were wealthy and self-sufficient. My mother had taught me that baby showers were vulgar, because they implied that people couldn't provide for their own and had to rely on others for gifts. Now it was time to ask for help. I had no choice. The baby was coming. I reached up and pressed the buzzer.

Suddenly, there was a flurry of activity as I was lifted on to the gurney, and Father Mike appeared. My face was twisting with pain and I cried out, "Help me, Father Mike, I feel like I'm dying."

As they wheeled me away to the delivery room, Father Mike was hanging over the gurney rail, sputtering, "My God, my God, my dearie darlin'! My angel! Don't worry! Don't worry about anything! I'm going to get us all set up in San Diego when this is over! I swear to you, don't worry about a thing! Oh, my God, my angel..." Then everything went black.

I became aware of the quiet. As I emerged from the inky darkness of gas anesthesia, I saw an unfamiliar face hanging over me. This was not my doctor. I said hazily, "Who are you?"

"I'm Doctor Stuart. I'm the doctor on duty."

"Oh, excuse me," I said, fighting to keep conscious, "but what did I have?"

"Girls like you don't want to know," he replied coldly.

His remark cut through me, but I pressed on. "I do want to know. Do you think you could just tell me if it's a boy or a girl?"

"It's a girl," he said, dryly.

"Is she healthy?" I asked.

"Yes, she's healthy, and that's all you need to know."

I sank back into a drugged twilight clutching his answer. A girl, our Dierdre.

After the birth, Father Mike somehow managed to get me a semi-private room. There awaited my next surprise: a black roommate. This new mother whose name was Elese was a twenty-six-year-old fifth grade schoolteacher in Phoenix. Having come from the South Side of Chicago and a family which was racially prejudiced, I had only encountered black people as servants. Now I was sharing this intimate, painful time with a black woman.

"Hello, I'm Elese. My baby boy was born yesterday. I'm so happy for you...Are you okay?"

"Oh yeah, thanks."

"Well, what did you have?

I swallowed. "I had a girl. She's healthy. Her name is Dierdre..." I felt I was in a haze. "Dierdre was to be killed at birth to save the kingdom...But she lived and news of her perfect beauty spread throughout the land..."

Elese added, "...and the Druid prophecy was that Dierdre would be forced to marry a king. I know that legend. It's sad, but lovely. But what a beautiful name. You seem tired, maybe you should rest."

"Thank you. I am tired. It must be these drugs they gave me..."

* * *

"Good morning, Royal. Are you feeling better now? They just brought breakfast and it was horrible. I don't think you missed anything," she laughed. "You were talking in your sleep last night."

"Oh yes, what was I saying?" I asked in surprise.

"Well, you kept repeating that you hadn't signed the papers

yet. You seemed worried about it. Can I help you with anything?"

"Uh...those drugs. They confused me."

"By the way, while you were sleeping Dierdre's grandfather came by."

My heart jumped. "How did you know her name?"

"Last night when they brought you in on the gurney, we talked about the Celtic legend of Dierdre. You don't remember?"

"Oh yeah, yeah I do. But,...grandfather? Was he an older Irish man with grey at the temples?"

She said, "Yes."

"Did he call himself Dierdre's grandfather?" I asked.

"No. I just assumed..."

"Well, Elese, that's Dierdre's father, and we have a big problem."

"I'm sorry I didn't mean to assume, or to pry."

"Oh no, that's okay. Since he's so much older my mother refuses to accept our marriage. He has convinced me that for the welfare of Dierdre, we may have to give her up for adoption."

"Oh dear, I'm so sorry. I hope you get to keep her."

I could sense her understanding my pain. She asked me if it would bother me to see her nursing her baby boy.

"Oh no, I think its wonderful you're nursing. I just wish my breasts could feed my baby, with all my heart I do."

* * *

Father Mike came to see me at appointed visiting hours but he was quiet and withdrawn. He seemed to be going through an agony of his own.

Nobody came to tell me anything about our baby. I started chewing out the insides of my mouth from the tension and the withheld emotion. I was fighting to hold myself together. I was afraid to open the door to my emotions; terrified Father Mike would leave me if I fell apart.

I never cried. Post-natal blues! Those hard blues. There was no counseling, there were no tranquilizers, nothing. My breasts were filling with milk, and I still had not seen my baby. I didn't even know where she was.

CHAPTER 20

After four days, the Catholic Social worker came to see me.

I said, "Could you tell me what happened to my baby, please?"

"Oh, your baby! I think it went home two days ago," she said, shuffling through some papers on her clipboard.

"Went home where?" I asked in alarm. "What home?"

"The babies go to a foster home first, and then..."

"But I haven't signed any adoption papers yet," I interrupted.

She looked flustered. "Oh, you haven't? Well, didn't they tell you the babies go to a foster home before they are adopted?"

"I don't remember that," I said.

"Okay. I'll be right back. I'm just going to check on this," she said, and nervously retreated.

I was astounded. I thought, this is a human being. This is my greatest gift to the world, and you don't even know where she is?

A few minutes later the social worker returned. "Your baby is still here," she said, sheepishly. "You didn't get to hold her yet?"

I shook my head.

"I'll bring her in so you can hold her."

"No!" My heart was pounding. "No, you may not bring the baby in for me to hold," I heard myself saying.

"What?" she asked, surprised.

"Do not bring my baby in here. Because if I hold her now, I will never let her go, and you will never have her."

All along Father Mike had refused to look at Dierdre, saying he didn't want to carry her image with him for the rest of his life. I understood this and I also hated him for it. Just before I left the hospital I asked Elese to accompany me to the nursery to look at her. She took my arm and together we made the painful journey down the tiled hall. Looking out of her plastic container from behind a glass window was my beautiful seven-and-a-half-pound Dierdre Dawn O'Donohoe. She was lying on her side swaddled tightly in a peach-colored blanket. The nursery room nurse had turned her to face me. She was pink and had a cherub face with blond fuzz on her head. She was perfect! She had the Phillips dimple in her left cheek. She was working her little lips as if she were hungry or preparing for a kiss. Then she opened her eyes and they seemed to lock onto mine. Love poured out of me. I wanted to grab her, hold her, smell her. I bit down hard on the inside of my mouth to control the despair and yearning that heaved in my breast as I looked upon this miracle. I felt torn apart, joined to her by an invisible magnet and wrenched away by Father Mike's decision that I must give her up. I had a fleeting impulse to shatter the glass partition, the transparent wall that thwarted my maternal instincts. I felt Elese's hand tighten on my arm.

"She's beautiful, Royal, like you," she said. She slipped her arm around me. "I think we'd better go now."

As I turned from the nursery I saw tears on Elese's face.

* * *

During the days following my release from the hospital, I was desperate. The lease on our apartment was about to expire. We were out of money. Dierdre was in a foster home, pending adoption. I still hadn't signed the papers. My body was recovering from childbirth, I had milk in my breasts and no baby to nurse. I was weak, depressed, and contaminated with unreleased emotion. Tears, the pain of broken dreams and betrayed trust, hopelessness and fear, all surged inside a tightly wrapped package, knotted with a cord I felt to be survival. I went day to day simply placing one foot in front of the other. I was numb.

CHAPTER 21

I reached deep inside myself and came up with my last-ditch plan, my last desperate attempt to find a way to keep Dierdre. I called my mother. Father Mike was vehemently against my plan but I ignored him and forged on. I was banking on her soft spot: the sense of "family blood" and pride that I knew was part of her Southern mentality. My mother loved babies—at least she loved her own grandchildren—and I thought maybe she would change her mind about Father Mike and me and help us stay together if she knew there was a baby, her own flesh and blood. I had nowhere else to turn.

"Royal, where the hell are you?"

"I'm in Arizona, Mother," I replied.

"Is that son of a bitch with you?" she snarled.

"Yes, he is."

"Are you pregnant?"

"No, I'm not. But I must tell you I love him and we want to stay together."

"Well, you may love him but as long as you are together you'll never be a part of my life or get any help from me. And I can assure you he will never again be a part of any life in Palm Springs.

I've seen to that. He's nothing but a dirty liar." There was an icy pause. "Listen Royal, I'm married now, and I can't be bothered by your problems. I have a new husband. An elderly gentleman named Mr. Hamilton, and I will not upset him. You've done enough. You've caused me nothing but pain and sorrow. I have a new life and I won't have it disturbed by your stupidity."

Her absence of caring, (she never once asked me how I was) her hatred and condemnation of Father Mike told me that there was no help to be found here.

My heart snapped shut. I thought, you cold bitch, you don't even deserve to know about your own flesh and blood." My last hopes turned to ash.

"You must want something from me. What is it?" I heard her shrill voice asking.

It was at this moment in the sweltering glass phone booth that I realized the family I was born into had nothing to offer me except material goods. I decided to stop fooling myself by expecting more. I would utilize their spiritless offerings, now.

"We've run out of money. I need a ticket home."

There was a short silence in which I could hear my mother relishing her triumph. "I expected this," she said. "You can come here on the condition that you come alone and do nothing, and I mean nothing to upset Mr. Hamilton or our household."

I said, "Of course, Mother."

I hung up the phone and walked toward Father Mike, who was waiting for me in the shade of the palm tree.

"Well?" he said.

"She offered me a ticket home."

Father Mike let me take a taxi to sign the adoption papers. The one thread of sanity that held me together was, that despite the nightmarish circumstances surrounding our lives, I felt I had accomplished something worthwhile. I had given the greatest gift to the world. A healthy baby. Right to the bitter end I had hung on to the idea that I would be able to keep her. I had no guilt about rejecting her because I never did. I never had the intention of giving her away. I cherished her to the end. I talked to her and loved her, loved her, loved her.

CHAPTER 22

I made a simple dinner for our apartment manager and his family to thank them for their kindness, and gave away the few household things we had. Father Mike's plan was for us to split up for a while. His only familiar base was the Church.

"Royal, I'm going to have to lie about us in order to re-enter the priesthood."

"The priesthood? You're not going back into the priesthood?" I asked.

"I have to go back. At least long enough to get myself reestablished..."

"But you're finally free. You've made a clean break."

He said, "This is only until I can get my financial affairs straightened out."

It was so frustrating to me that he could come up with no other solution to our tragic predicament than to return to the hypocrisy he had left behind.

"I have a friend in Blythe..."

"Isn't that on the California-Arizona border?"

"Yes...who will put me up until I contact the Bishop. I'll

probably be required to go on retreat at Via Coeli Monastery in New Mexico."

"How do you know?" I asked.

"From my former experience of re-entering the priesthood. Remember I'm an old hand at this," he said sarcastically. "I'll have to do penance to cleanse my soul."

"Cleanse your soul? Do you really believe that?"

"Now Royal, don't be startin' with that again."

He claimed he loved me and he begged me to give him some time. He responded to my deepening depression by promising we could have more babies when we were together again and stable.

* * *

As a dog returneth to his vomit,

So a fool returneth to his folly.

Proverbs 26:11

We each returned to the familiar. We took a small plane, a puddle-jumper, out of Phoenix. Father Mike got off in Blythe; I got off in Palm Springs. I carried the oil paintings I had done in Spain wrapped in brown paper under my arms.

Returning to Palm Springs was like going in front of a firing squad.

My mother's first words to me were, "You're as fat as ever. You look like S-H-I-T." She actually believed she would remain a lady if she only spelled these words.

On the way to the "The Marble Crypt" I saw flowers wilting in the desert heat but was chilled by the approach of my mother's domain. She laid down the rules of my re-entry.

"Now, Royal, you will have to behave correctly around Mr. Hamilton. You must respect him at all times as he is an older gentleman."

"And how old might that be, Mother?"

"That is none of your business, young lady. And another thing...I don't want you playing your music loudly on your Hi-Fi."

"Oh, you mean to say, I still have a Hi-Fi?" I asked.

"Watch that tone of voice, Royal. I won't put up with that. Wipe that smug look off your face. You no longer have your MG. I sold it as soon as you left. Remember you are not coming into this home under the best of circumstances."

"Yes, Mother."

She had rebounded from my disappearance by marrying Mr. Hamilton, donating a stained glass window to the Church to wipe clean her slate, and buying a new Cadillac. Mr. Hamilton, whose first name I later learned was Wendell—although my mother never referred to him as anything but Mr. Hamilton—was eighty-one years old and frail as a teacup.

While I was unpacking my things he came toward me pointing his bony white finger, "You'd better behave yourself here," he said. "We know what you've done, young lady. We had you followed."

This presumptuous, tottering ghost had obviously been

131

primed by my mother. I had no idea if he meant they knew about Dierdre or not. I learned from him that private detectives had tracked us to Phoenix and were still nosing around on our trail there. I had told no one about my baby, except Christine, and Father Mike had made me vow that I never would. Her existence would be our sacred secret.

I talked to no one in Palm Springs, not even the Chandlers. I was living in a vacuum, having nightmares about the baby and hiding my grief from everyone. My breasts were swollen with milk, a reminder of the cycle that would never be completed. The insides of my mouth were now raw and bleeding. My mother had adopted a new façade along with her new husband. When sober, she was in total denial of the past. As usual, we were going to pretend that nothing had happened. At least to the outside world. She forbade me to mention Father Mike's name.

"The S.O.B. has cost you your inheritance," she told me. "What has happened is over, Royal, and I don't want the shameful incident mentioned again in my home. I'll know the whole truth soon enough when I get the detective's final report."

CHAPTER 23

Part of washing away the past for my mother was insisting that I go to confession. "I'm taking you to church for confession," she said. "I have made a private appointment for you. However, not at Saint Theresa's Parish where that S.O.B. was living a lie."

My inner reaction was, "This is ridiculous! What a sham!"

But she was relentless. Finally I gave in to appease her. In my confusion and grief I was frantically reaching for some kind of help.

On some level, the confessional was better than nothing. She took me to Our Lady of Sorrows, the smallest of all the Catholic churches in Palm Springs, attended mostly by Agua Caliente Indians. She had donated most of the windows there.

Alone in the church, I was greeted by a calm coolness and the familiar smell of incense and candles. I walked to the statue of the Virgin and lit a votive candle for Dierdre. Kneeling in the dark confessional box, I began timidly, "Bless me, Father, for I have sinned. My last confession was..."

"Where is he? Are you pregnant?" The priest's voice boomed from the other side of the mesh screen. I was stunned by the interruption of this holy ritual. The safety of the confessional is one of the oldest and most sacred traditions of the Roman Catholic Church. As I digested what was happening, I realized this priest wanted to rat on Father Mike to the Bishop. It was all a point system: one point for having something on him; two, for being the first to turn him in. I was horrified. I had gone in there with a thread of hope that I would be comforted. I needed to speak my pain. I desperately needed to lay down my burdens before someone I could trust. I needed help. Because I had nowhere else to turn, I had given the Church one more chance. At his words, a cold curtain fell across my heart and I reclaimed ownership of my soul.

I arose from my knees and said loudly, "To answer your questions, I am not pregnant and I don't know where he is. Thanks for hearing my confession," I added bitterly.

Fighting back rage, I stumbled through the dimness out into the glaring sunlight, where my mother was waiting for me in her new baby blue Cadillac.

* * *

The days that followed were a blur. I alternated between numbness and unbearable despair. When drunk, my mother forgot her muzzle and, backed by Mr. Hamilton, stirred the ashes of the past and seized every opportunity to remind me that I was good for nothing.

Often during the day, the last nine months seemed no more than an eerie blue dream. But at night, when I was alone and tossing sleeplessly in my bed, when the pain in my engorged breasts brought back the truth, reality flew in and perched at the foot of my bed like an ominous black crow. Then I would be haunted by images of Spain, of Phoenix, and of Dierdre's face. I would reach out to comfort my phantom child and suddenly find myself a small child, helpless and alone, locked in my bedroom on Pleasant Avenue, in Chicago.

I was struggling for an anchor between dream and reality. I thought of my trunk and the dreams of a happy future it once contained. I needed to see what was in there. I reached through my solitary confinement and called Ramona Chandler. I asked her to take me to Redlands to get the trunk that had never been sent to Spain. From the garage of Harold White's house, the housekeeper, Ramona and I hoisted the trunk into the back seat of the car. In the safety of Ramona's house, we opened my trunk of broken dreams. As we unpacked the cookbooks, the baby clothes, and the baby blankets that I had knitted, all of the disappointment and loss, the yearning and helplessness I had buried came exploding to the surface and for the first time, I cried. I cried for myself, I cried for my baby, and I cried for Father Mike.

Ramona held me in her arms. I finally felt safe. Without consulting Father Mike, without consulting anything other than my irrepressible need to let go, I sobbed out my story to her. Finally, my heart-wrenching pain released.

"Oh, Honey, I don't know how you've lived through this. My heart is just breaking for you," she said.

"I haven't told anyone anything, Ramona, and I don't think my mother knows. She has had her detectives after us but I don't know if they'll find out about the baby. So promise me you will keep this secret."

"Of course, I will honey, you know I'd never break your trust. Cyril and I only want to see you happy."

"Father Mike said he was going back into the Church to try and get his finances together. I guess without me and without the baby, he thought he could maneuver more easily. But now I don't even know where he is. I believe he loves me, Ramona, but sometimes I'm just so confused. All I wanted was for us to get away from here and be who we really are," I sobbed.

"He must have a plan for you, honey," she said, wiping my tears with her hand. "He couldn't possibly have just left you."

"I just don't know what he's going to do and I don't know what I am going to do. I'm frantic, Ramona. I can't stand living with my mother anymore. I'm going crazy. I've even thought about joining the Army or the Navy, you know, becoming a WAC or a WAVE or maybe I could be a nanny. I just don't know where to go, but I have to get out of here."

"I wish I could help you more, my dear Royal," she said as she stroked me. "You know how Cyril and I love you, but your mother is so unpredictable with her drinking, I'm afraid of the trouble she could cause us if we tried to interfere."

My mother had always resented my friendship with the Chandlers and did a poor job of covering her jealousy so I understood their reluctance to be involved.

CHAPTER 24

A week later, Father Mike finally called. My mother was drunk. Thank God I answered the phone. He quickly gave me his phone number and I dashed down to Palm Canyon Drive to call him from a phone booth.

"Father Mike, where are you? You've got to get me out of here!" I cried hysterically. "I'm going to go crazy. I'm going to kill myself or better yet I'm going to kill my mother. That bitch keeps calling me a whore! She tells me I'm good for nothing. And these rules. I'm living like a prisoner in here! I can't breath! I can't stand it! Something terrible is going to happen. If you love me, Father Mike, you'll get me out of here."

Father Mike's voice was irritated. "Now calm down, Royal, just hang on. You know I love you but I'm not in a position yet to have you with me. I'm going to need to figure this out."

"Well, for God's sake, where are you, Father Mike?" I shouted.

"I'm not far away and don't ask me any more questions! I want you to just sit tight while I try to arrange something. You've got to understand this isn't the way I planned it and it's dangerous for me right now, dangerous for both of us."

"I can't wait much longer, Father Mike. I told you she's making me crazy. I'll do as you say, but if you don't hurry one of us will be dead."

"Then call me at five on Friday."

"You'll work something out by then?" I asked, doubting his words.

"I'll try my best to have some news for you. I know a woman near here who may be able to help us."

* * *

I had several more conversations with Father Mike over the next few days, while he worked out a plan for me to leave Palm Springs. When he was ready, he asked me to take the Greyhound bus to Ontario, a town an hour and a half west of Palm Springs, but I was overwhelmed and weak and couldn't face riding a bus.

"I just can't do it, Father Mike," I told him. "I haven't slept. I'm too nervous and for God's sake I still have milk in my breasts. Why can't you just come get me?"

I finally talked him into driving to Palm Springs to pick me up. We arranged to meet at night at the Greyhound bus station on Indian Avenue.

I packed my things while my mother lunged drunkenly in and out of my room. She hurled, "You slut! You whore! You're nothing but a whore."

I screamed back, "This time I'm leaving for good, you crazy bitch! You won't be bothered by me any more...this is it. I must have been out of my mind to think I could come back to live here. God, look at you in those stupid men's pajamas."

"How dare you take the Lord's name in vain, you whore!"

"Shut up! I'm tired of hearing your drunken insults. There has never been any love between us and there never will be."

"Ha! What do you know about love? You've never loved me!"

I screamed back, "That's not true! I've tried to love you all my life, but you can't see it through your demented Bourbon eyes."

She swung her arm around, spilling her drink, to point and say, "How dare you accuse me...of me being drunk. You're going straight to hell!"

"Well, you're lucky I'm leaving now, or I'd be going to hell for killing you."

"I said, you're going to hell! You stupid...fat...whore! You won't get a penny from me."

"But, mother, this is hell...and I'm leaving."

* * *

The first words I heard from Father Mike were, "This is sheer foolishness, my coming to Palm Springs, when you could have taken the bus. Don't you realize the risk I am taking by having contact with you now."

"I know I am an inconvenience to you right now, Father Mike, but I had no other choice. Look at the inside of my mouth," I said, pulling back my cheeks to show him the open raw flesh. "Look at my hands, they're shaking. I had to get out of there," I cried. "Where was I to go? You may be able to back-peddle into your old life but I've changed. I can't go back."

"Don't you see, my brainless girl, I'm doing this not because I want to but because it is the only thing I know. I am doing this so we can have a life together later. I love you, but don't you see, I'm in the middle of re-entry. I asked you for some time. I'm not having an easy go of it either. You should see the god-forsaken parish they've laid on me now. You're not going to be able to stay in this area for very long. I wish you would take my suggestion and go to San Diego, where I have friends who could help you get started.

As we drove on to Ontario Father Mike told me what had transpired in the last few weeks. He had properly repented and had done what was required of him by the Diocese to re-enter the priesthood.

"Exactly how did you repent, Father Mike?"

"I told them that I had fled to Spain, as a result of a personal crisis of faith."

"Did you tell them that you were alone?"

"Yes. Of course I did. What would you have me tell them? I said I had been tapped out and could no longer serve my parishioners in a condition of doubt."

"In a way that was true. You were sick of the hypocrisy. I suppose you told them you wrote your memoirs."

He at looked me in surprise. "How would you be knowin' that?"

"I know you better than you think. You always said I was dumb like a fox."

He said he had utilized the time to write his memoirs of his time as a chaplain in the Korean war. He never admitted having lived with me or having had Dierdre.

I suspected that his quick re-acceptance into the priesthood was based on his reputation as a dynamic money maker. They had demoted him to pastor of San Secondo d'Asti Church in Guasti, formally known as South Cucamonga. It was the smallest parish in all of Southern California in the middle of a dusty vineyard.

He said, "I know a widow in Ontario, a few miles from Guasti, who is willing to harbor you."

"Harbor me?"

"Yes, harbor you, you can't be particular now. You have no choice."

"I'm aware of my lack of options. Thank you for reminding me."

I felt myself dangling on the end of a wire over a dark abyss. Father Mike's affection and warmth that had fed me for so long were eclipsed by his absorption in his own problems. I had become a burden to him now. I didn't know if I had the stamina to go on alone. I was sinking.

CHAPTER 25

The Ontario widow, who had been told she was sheltering me from an "unhealthy family environment," opened the door of her ranch-style tract house, squinted her eyes to take us both in and then reached out a hand laden with large pink rings and pulled Father Mike toward her. While hugging him, she examined me over his shoulder. I couldn't imagine what their connection could be.

The widow appeared to be in her early sixties, had bleached blond hair, smoked incessantly, and was never without a tumbler of creme de menthe. After Father Mike left I felt uncomfortable and displaced. I retreated to her back guest room and tried to keep out of her way. Around five p.m. she came to my room and announced that my dinner was ready. Surprised, I asked if I could help her with dinner preparations.

"Oh no, I don't ever eat this early," she said. "I've just made something for you."

In the middle of the table directly under an avocado-green and orange mosaic chandelier, sat a dusty bowl of plastic fruit. My solitary dinner was on a place mat depicting the Empire State Building. The widow sat down with her glass of creme de menthe to watch me eat. Dinner was a bowl of lukewarm Campbell's chicken noodle soup, made with milk instead of water.

After politely gagging down my soup, I went back to the guest room and tried to keep myself from falling apart. Several times I heard my hostess talking to people who weren't there.

About ten o'clock I got ready for bed. I had a red velvet robe from Saks 5th Avenue with a white Peter Pan collar and white lace on the sleeves. I put it on and finished unpacking my dresses. I heard the widow bumping down the hallway toward my room, her ice cubes clinking. She was already engaged in conversation with the Invisible Ones. When she reached the door, her eyes widened. She was staring at my robe.

"Take off my robe!" she demanded.

"What? This is my robe," I said, shocked.

"It's not your robe. It's my robe. You're stealing my robe," she slurred accusingly.

I sat there mutely trying to figure out what she was talking about. "I'm afraid you're confused." I said. "This is my own robe. Do you have one like it? Maybe we have the same robe," I offered.

She lurched toward me and sloshing sticky green liqueur on her pants suit, plucked at the sleeve of my robe. "You couldn't possibly have the same robe. My robe came from Saks 5th Avenue!"

CHAPTER 26

As a last resort, Father Mike brought me to his tiny room adjoining the whitewashed chapel in Guasti. To the right of the white marble altar was a door opening directly into his room, which contained a bed with a medal headboard painted to look like wood, a dresser, and one small wooden pew. The chapel was within a stone's throw of the railroad tracks and at night, as we lay crammed together in the tiny metal bed, we would be awakened by the vibration of the passing freight trains.

When I would start to cry or make a fuss about our impossible living situation, Father Mike would try to appease me by making love to me. But it was no longer the joyous lovemaking of the past; now it was riddled with fear of getting caught, and fear of my getting pregnant again. We were frightened all the time. Father Mike was trying to figure out what to do with me.

On Sundays, he said Mass at eight and ten a.m. I was instructed to stay out of sight. From a crack in our door, I could see him in his vestments, fifteen feet away, giving his sermon from the carved wooden pulpit. I could see the attentive faces of his first-row parishioners, the simple grape pickers of the Guasti fields.

After one day of his preaching, I asked, "Father Mike how can you stand the hypocrisy of what you teach? You talk about purity while I'm hiding out in the next room, waiting for our next screw."

"Oh, screwing is it? I loathe that term. I thought we were

144

making love, Royal."

"I don't know what we're doing anymore. I don't know anything, any more. All I know is that I have to get out of here. This is insane."

"Now, now, settle down. Lower your voice you're getting loud. Do you want me thrown out of even this parish?"

That night, I again rejected Father Mike's suggestion that I go to San Diego. I decided I had to leave. I had two hundred dollars that Ramona and Cyril had loaned me.

"I think you should use that money to go to San Diego, Royal. I can help you get set up there. I know people there. I am still trying to get ahold of 'dependable Harold' and when I do, I'll send you some money."

"Don't hold your breath on that one, Father Mike. When I went to get my trunk there was only a maid who didn't speak a word of English. And as far as San Diego goes, you may know people there but I don't and I am not going there."

* * *

I was facing the terrifying realization that I alone was going to decide what to do with my life. And I had to do it fast.

I had often thought that if I could pick any place in the world to live, my first choice would be Santa Barbara. I had fallen in love with it while visiting Doug there during vacations from University of New Mexico. I called Doug at his parent's home and was surprised to find him there. He had dropped out of college and was working for his father. He was surprised to hear from me. I sidestepped his questions, promising to fill him in later, if he would agree to meet me at the bus station and help me find an apartment. I made plans to leave. Father Mike continued to promise me that we would have a life together in the future, but his words were no longer the life preservers they had once been. As much as I loved him, I just couldn't hang on to the promise of reviving our shattered past. My survival instincts dictated that I simply move forward for myself now.

Father Mike and I kissed each other good-bye in his car, which he had parked behind the bus station where we wouldn't be seen.

* * *

I boarded the bus for Los Angeles with one white Samsonite suitcase, and a clock radio. I had in my purse the two hundred dollars from the Chandlers and an envelope from Father Mike containing forty-three one-dollar bills "borrowed" from the collection plate. I had no idea what I was going to do in Santa Barbara. I was just going to the next place.

I wasn't ready for the Greyhound bus station in downtown L.A. It was a sleazy hub for a cross section of humanity, travelers of every sort and criminal characters going nowhere. Waiting for my bus to Santa Barbara, I sat on a bench tightly clutching my purse and chewing the insides of my mouth. I prayed to God that the pair of wiry, tattooed Mexicans who had been eyeing me for the last twenty minutes would vanish. Instead, the one that looked like Sal Mineo slid onto the bench next to me.

"I get you anything you want. You want drugs? I get you. No problem. What you want?" he whispered.

I was floored. I was too frightened to speak. I grew rigid, stiffly turned away and pretended he wasn't there. When he finally left, I picked up my suitcase and clock radio and headed for the safety of the ladies room but before I had gotten ten steps I was approached by a persistent sailor who wanted to buy me a drink in the bar. He said I looked like Kim Novac and he'd be mighty pleased if I'd do him the honor before he shipped out to San Diego.

I made it to the restroom where I cowered until my bus to Santa Barbara was announced. An Oriental mother came in behind me toting a crying little girl dressed in a crumpled pink satin costume with a glitter crown crafted out of pipe cleaners. I wondered if my Dierdre would ever dress-up and pretend. Then I looked at the little girl's shopping bag of candy and realized it was Halloween. I thought, everyday is Halloween in the L.A. bus depot.

CHAPTER 27

The interior of the bus was dark, and though I fought sleep I was lulled by the steady hum of the engine. Weeks of anxiety and fitful nights left me prey to the surging tendrils of sleep that waited to encircle me like a cocoon. I let my armor slide away into the empty seat next to me and sank into a spongy oblivion.

The smell of salty sea air pulled me out of my soothing reverie. It was night. We had reached the Rincon, a long sweeping corner of the coast about twenty miles south of Santa Barbara, where the road follows the contour of the sea and waves wrap around the point rolling in, their cadence echoing across the highway. From the window, I saw the breakers illuminated with the neon glow of phosphorescence, sparkling like fireworks on the Fourth of July. I didn't try to unravel the mystery of this natural magic. I simply pressed my head against the cold glass and watched it and felt calm. As the bus passed the little town of Summerland, I could see the lights of the Santa Barbara harbor twinkling in the distance. Although I didn't know where I was headed in my life, I felt as though I had made the right decision coming to this place. I felt safe, cradled between ocean and mountains.

Within a day and a half, I had found a furnished studio for fifty-five dollars a month at the end of Valerio Street near the 101 Highway. Once again I began with only the bare necessities. I bought one set of plastic Blue Willow dishes and a cast iron frying pan from Woolworth's and one set of sheets and a blanket from Montgomery Ward.

I knew already that Doug would not be a part of my future. He had met me at the bus station with a six pack of beer and driven me down to Hendry's beach where we sat and talked in the parking lot overlooking the ocean. He grumbled about working for a father whom he thought hated him. And Doug seemed to be more afraid of him than ever. I told him about Father Mike and me, about Dierdre's birth and about the pain of giving her up for adoption.

When I began to cry, he put his head in his hands. "Don't cry. For God's sakes, don't cry, Kitten. I just can't handle it," he said.

I knew for sure then that we would never have made it, that he could never have withstood the pressures from my mother or his father. He could not be there for me, so once again I reeled in my emotions and marched on as if in a dream.

I knew I had to find a job right away, and scanning the want-ads of the Santa Barbara News-Press, I saw that the Blue Onion Restaurant, just a few blocks away needed a cocktail waitress. I figured, with a Fine Arts education that was about the best I could do for the time being. I walked into the manager's office the next afternoon and he hired me on the spot. I was more concerned about the uniform than the pay. I concluded that if I lowered the hem a few inches it would be okay. After a week and a half of pretending to ignore ogling glances down the bodice of my uniform and the cries of infants in the restaurant, I could no longer bear the reminders that I was a mother and had lost my baby. It was a pain that never left me.

I reached for the only person I could talk to: Ramona.

"Ramona, I'm in Santa Barbara...Father Mike has been

demoted to the Guasti Parish. You know the little church in the middle of the vineyards?...He wanted me to go to San Diego, but I had to come here. He was so mean to me, you have no idea," I said as I began to cry. "I don't want to live any more. I just simply can't take any more. I can't go on!"

I could barely hear her, so I asked, "What?...my mother called you?...Oh you think she might help me, huh? Was she sober?..." I gave Ramona permission to tell her where I was.

The next week, I was awakened one morning at six by the loud ring of my party line. It could only have been one person.

"Hello, Royal, it's Mother."

"Yes, I can tell it's you, Mother."

"Well, I hear from Ramona that you're alone. Is this true?"

"Yes, Mother. I'm here in Santa Barbara by myself," I sighed.

"Well, I'm certainly glad to hear that. You're not getting back together with that good for nothing Doug, I hope," she said.

"No Mother, I'm not," I sighed wearily, rubbing the soles of my sore feet together, under the sheets. "I came here to start a new life."

"That sounds fine, Royal, but what are you going to do? And how are you going to support yourself?"

"I have a job," I said, dreading what was to come. "I have a job as a cocktail waitress in a restaurant."

"A cocktail waitress?" she exploded. "You can't be a cocktail waitress! For God's sake, a cocktail waitress!"

"Well, I have been for two weeks now," I said defensively.

"You're never going to amount to anything doing that," her voice rose. "How do you expect to meet a decent man in a bar?"

"Then what do you suggest I do, Mother?"

"Well, you could go to a business school like I did. At least you'd learn some acceptable skills to support yourself."

I looked at my crumpled uniform lying on the floor beside the bed where I had stepped out of it, exhausted, the night before. I didn't need much convincing to take her advice. I was running on empty. Be realistic, I thought. Take what she has to offer.

"Okay, Mother," I said. "You send the money and I'll go to business school."

I enrolled in the Santa Barbara Business College, three miles from my apartment. My classmates were mostly young women my age who had college degrees in things like archeology or philosophy and had found them useless in the business workaday environment of the early 1960s, where women were still expected to fill stereotypical roles.

I attended classes six hours a day and I walked everywhere. Going home, up State Street, I'd look at the baby dolls in the windows of Woolworth's and I'd burst into tears. Then I started ordering scotch delivered to my little apartment from Roy's Liquor Store on Haley Street. Coming to Santa Barbara all by myself was like coming out of jail without a parole officer to report to. I was on my own.

To the outside world, to my TEACHERS and fellow students, my story was that I had been in Spain studying art, and before that at the University of New Mexico. Once again, I was living a lie and my secrets isolated me.

CHAPTER 28

On my way home from business college, I was often drawn into
Woolworth's by the garish window displays of metal foot lockers
and plastic Christmas trees. I would wander around aimlessly,
fascinated by the vast array of knick-knacks open to inspection in
huge glass partitioned bins. I meandered between bins of plastic
coin purses, nail polish, wooden spools of thread and skeins of
variegated yarn. I idly sifted through cotton socks and scarves
emblazoned with tourist motifs.

In the back of the store was the pet section. I visited
Woolworth many times before I could comfortably venture
through the aisles of chattering parakeets and red-eyed white mice
sleeping on top of each other.

I felt relatively calm in the presence of the gold fish and
wanted to buy two of them for company. I took them home in a
little white cardboard container, the kind used for Chinese take-out.
I also bought a bowl, gravel for the bottom, some seaweed, a net
and fish flakes. These were my first fish. I named them Bogart
and Bacall. When their bowl grew dark green with algae, I set out
the implements for changing their water: a Pyrex dish with fresh
water, and the net. Then I prepared to scoop them up and move
them to the Pyrex dish so I could clean their bowl. I was
unprepared for how they would react when caught in the net.
Their fat little orange bodies flipped frantically, as they gasped for
air. Their terror and gasping frightened me and my hand froze,

poised above their bowl, as I stared, horrified, before plunging them back into their murky water. I couldn't do it. The responsibility of taking them, however briefly, out of water, was more than I could handle. I sat down to think. Why was I plagued by all these fears? Why couldn't I behave like normal people did? I had been through so much in my life that was abnormal, why then were these normal encounters so difficult for me? I didn't have an answer. I sat there watching Bogart and Bacall floundering in the murk and poured myself a glass of scotch. After awhile I felt fortified by the Johnny Walker and was able to suppress my fear enough to do what I had to do. I moved Bogart and Bacall into the Pyrex dish and back into the comfort of a clean bowl.

In the future, I had a couple of drinks before the then brave weekly changing of the fish bowl.

* * *

The party line rang one weekend. And I was surprised to find my brother, Merv, calling from New Jersey.

"Royal, Mother gave me your number. I want to come out to see you."

"You do?" I asked. "You really want to see me?...You know what I've done, don't you?"

"Why, yes. Don't you know how worried we've been about you?"

"I had no idea. Mother told me that I was disowned... disinherited...diseverything."

"I have a business trip in L.A. next weekend, and I will come up to see you."

When my brother took me out to dinner, after we both had many drinks, I blurted out my story. He did not condemn me or damn me. I felt secure enough to share my secret. He promised me he would not break my trust. Together we wept in each other's arms. It was the first time I ever saw my big brother cry.

CHAPTER 29

My drinking only depressed me more and left me with severe hangovers. I would awake early with a splitting headache and diarrhea, feeling jittery and anxious. I had very few friends. Doug had faded away. Occasionally I was invited to the homes of my classmates, but I never really opened up to anyone, I never told any of my girlfriends about Father Mike and I kept my sacred secret about Dierdre.

And to that degree I remained in a separate world. I could see nothing in my future but emptiness. After business college, I would probably end up in a small Santa Barbara office as a typist or a file clerk.

It was Christmas time and I longed for some word from Father Mike. It was too dangerous to call him and knowing he was under the scrutiny of the Church, he had forbidden me to write him. We had agreed to use Ramona as a go-between but as far as I knew, he hadn't contacted her.

I wondered where Dierdre was spending her first Christmas. I began to wonder if Father Mike had ever really loved me. Had he led me on with the promise of marriage simply out of his fear that his soul would be damned if I had an abortion? Had he avoided destroying an embryo only to reject the child in the end? I wondered if he had really sent in a resignation to the Bishop or had he just taken some kind of leave of absence.

I became haunted by misgivings. The pain and hopelessness of my life was caving in on me and I began to think about suicide. I had no pills, so it would have to be gas. I thought about putting Bogart and Bacall on the outside doorstep, turning on the jets of the gas stove in my closet-like kitchen, closing the door and just going to sleep there. I would lie down on the floor with my pillow and simply never wake up again. I knew I could never do anything violent that would leave a mess for someone else to clean up.

I drank more. And more and more I found myself entertaining these morbid thoughts.

During this time my mother forwarded me a fat letter from my old wild childhood friend, Piper North. Its contents were shocking. The girl who had referred to herself in high school as the Holy Roman Empress of the World had decided to become a Roman Catholic nun. This was at the

very same time as I was believing in the Irish priest.

My mother called frequently, drunk and sober, to check on my progress in Business College. I think she was having some kind of trouble with Mr. Hamilton, though she never revealed anything specific.

She surprised me with an offer to buy me a car for Christmas.

"What about a Volkswagen Bug?" I asked.

"Those ugly beetle looking cars? You would want something like that."

"But I think they're cute. I like them and they don't cost much. That's what I want."

"You may never park that grotesque piece of machinery in front of my house. I will only buy you a Karman Ghia."

A few days before Christmas, I went to Van Wyck's Volkswagen and picked out a blue and white coupe, and right away my life began to brighten. It was Christmas break at the business college and a friend in my typing class suggested we drive over the San Marcos Pass into the valley past Solvang and up to Figueroa Mountain. This was my first trip outside the city. We descended the pass into the sensuous green rolling hills of the valley, dotted with stately live oaks. On the right lay Lake Cachuma, its blue inlets stretching toward us like welcoming fingers.

As the road turned to dirt and we reached the sugar pine trees on Figueroa Mountain, our car startled a cow which must have been lying near the side of the road. She seemed to be injured and had trouble moving. We saw a red cellophane-looking substance clinging to her flanks, as she turned and waddled into taller grass. I stopped the car. When we got out, we saw her newborn calf, still wet, lying in the grass just a few feet away. Startled by us, it struggled to stand and took its first steps on wobbly legs. I couldn't believe my eyes. I felt we had stumbled onto a miracle. I choked back tears and chewed my mouth as we returned to the car. Coming home at twilight, we dropped down the pass into the Christmas sparkle of the city. It reminded me so much of Spain, of coming down into Málaga on the Costa del Sol. The lights on the giant Christmas trees lining State Street danced in the crisp sea air. I rolled down the window and inhaled the smell of fresh pine. I was falling in love with my new home.

On Christmas Eve, I took a bubble bath, put on my red robe and sat down in front of Bogart and Bacall to eat the pre-cooked turkey breast I had purchased along with a cheap bottle of Champagne at Jordano's Supermarket. Johnny Mathis sang Christmas songs on the clock radio. I cried myself to sleep.

I woke up with a headache and wondered how I would get through Christmas day. The few friends I had were busy with their families. I got up and made some sandwiches, thinking I would drive back up into the mountains. I cleaned up the clutter from the night before and carried the sandwiches and a six-pack of beer in a pillow case out to my car. Out of the corner of my eye I saw a male figure walking on the next block squinting at street numbers, apparently lost. Something in his gait attracted my attention and watching him approach, I realized it was Father Mike. I felt an initial wave of surprise and excitement, followed by a dulling apprehension.

"Father Mike, is that you?" I called out.

His round face lit up and his steps quickened as he rushed toward me. "None other. And you'd be the very one I'm looking for," he said, embracing me and planting an energetic kiss on my lips.

"I can't believe ... Why are you ... What are you doing here?" I stammered.

"I'm here to see you, my dearie darlin'. Why else do you think I'd be peering up and down this bleary street?"

"How did you know how to find me?"

"I'm always going to know how to find you!"

"No, come on Father Mike, really, how did you find me?" I asked seriously. "Did Ramona tell you?"

"Yes, and it was no easy task getting it out of her. I practically had to sign a pledge of honorable intentions."

"That might not be such a bad idea," I said, slinging the picnic sack into the back of the car. "This is my Christmas present from Mother," I said, indicating my Karman Ghia with a sweeping gesture. "I was just about to go for a drive. Hop in and I'll take you on a picnic."

Father Mike looked a bit surprised but said, "I'm glad you're taking advantage of what the old souse has to offer."

He grabbed his jacket and a bottle of Liebfraumilch, a gift for me, from his rental car and we headed north up the coast on Highway 101.

On the drive, I pelted him with questions about his Guasti church, about his attempts to reach Harold White and about his plans for the future. I found out he had left Guasti two weeks ago. He had left the Church again! He was now in Mount Shasta where he said he hoped to start up a Haul-It-Yourself business with some old friends.

"I couldn't stand being in that dreadful, dreary little church any longer," he told me, opening a beer. "They were really rubbing my nose in it," he added bitterly.

Lacking true penitence, he had found the punishment unbearable and had fled again. Harold White was home from his travels and broke.

"What do you think you're going to do now?" I asked.

"If everything goes according to plan up north, we should have a fleet of trucks on the road and be sitting pretty by next year. I have my eye on a new Thunderbird that I know you would look a treat in," he said, passing me the can of beer.

"Who are these people in Mount Shasta, Father Mike?" I asked. "You never mentioned them before when we were in Phoenix."

"My darlin', I have known and lost touch with people all over the country in my years as a priest. I had lost touch with these but they are trustworthy friends and this is a first-class operation. I'm lucky to be in on it and if all goes well, it will secure our future," he said, squeezing my shoulder.

I exited the highway at the El Capitan State Park turnoff and headed for the beach. The wooded beach-front park was deserted. We ate our sandwiches on a picnic table overlooking the ocean. Brown pelicans pierced the glassy surface, dive-bombing for fish. We finished the six pack and Father Mike ceremoniously opened the wine and toasted our future. For a moment I saw him tanned and jolly, theatrically mixing drinks in my mother's Palm Springs cabana. I told him what had transpired in my life since Guasti and how sad I'd been. I wanted to talk about Dierdre but he cut me off.

He put his arm around me and drew me to him. "I want you to put all the bad behind you, now, darlin'. Our future is looking very bright."

While elaborating on his grandiose plans, he drained the bottle of wine and suggested we get another on the way home. This drinking pattern was familiar to me. I looked at his rumpled Countess Mara tie. Behind all the bravado I saw a confused, desperate man. He was more lost than I was. He had left the Church in what I thought was an attempt to live honestly and I respected that, but he never made a clean break. He had always kept the door open. Lacking the courage and confidence to walk away from his old life, he had denied himself the power necessary to create a new one. As much as I wanted to believe in him, I was no longer seduced by his words. He never once spoke

of our Dierdre or asked how I was.

We watched the sun set and the sky turn from cerulean to pale pink. On the drive home, Father Mike chattered cheerfully recounting anecdotes about his friends in Shasta while I listened in silence. We stopped for more wine and when Father Mike got back in the car I asked him if he had any rubbers.

"Well now, its not something I'm accustomed to having with me," he replied, rather taken aback.

"Well, I think you had better get some if you're thinking of romping with me."

"Romping with you is the very thing I'm always thinking of," he teased. "So you best be taking me to a drug store immediately then."

Cradled in Father Mike's arms, I sought the comfort and strength I had so often found there. I tasted his familiar kisses and inhaled the closeness of him. I closed my eyes and tried to recreate the excitement I had felt with this man who, a year ago, was leading me to an exhilarating new life. I tried to match my passion to his, to join again in his dreams for our future. But I found only an echo of emptiness.

The next morning I woke up irritable and on edge. My sleep had been restless and plagued by bad dreams. Father Mike and I both had slight hangovers. I made tea and scrambled up Mexican eggs with salsa while he took a shower. Sitting down to eat, Father Mike commented on my jittery mood. I told him I still thought a lot about Dierdre and wondered what kind of people she had ended up with. I told him I thought often about killing myself.

"Can we not leave that behind us?" Father Mike snapped. "There is nothing to gain by wallowing in the past. Dierdre's in a good home. We have to let that be and look to the future."

"But how do you know she's in a good home? Do you know more than I do?" I asked, pinning him with my eyes.

"All I know is that the Catholic Social Services would have found her a good home. That's their job," he sighed. "You must hear me now, she is no longer our child, Royal. You have to get that through your head. She has new parents. Its over and I will not discuss her anymore. We should look to the future. We will have more children together."

"No other child will ever replace this one, Father Mike," I said, turning on him. "And I refuse to keep quiet about it. Who do you want me to talk to about her if not you? Am I supposed to keep it buried inside me for the rest of my life? I think about her all the time. I can't forget her. She's a part of me," I said angrily.

"I know that, Royal," he replied softly. "I'm just asking you to bury the past."

"But the past has happened, Father Mike. How could I ever trust you enough to have more children? I believed that you loved me, that we would be married, that we would be a family and none of it ever happened. Sometimes I wonder if you really intended to marry me, or were you just afraid of going to hell if I had an abortion?"

Father Mike looked at me in amazement. "You know I don't believe in abortion, if that's what you're getting at. And God knows I did intend to marry you. It was your bleary-eyed mother who threw a wrench into everything. You know that as well as I do. I won't live or raise a child living like a pauper. I have a chance now to really make some money and if this Haul-It-Yourself business in Shasta works out we'll be financially secure and I can provide us with the kind of life we deserve."

"Okay. But how trustworthy are these people, Father Mike? How can they be such good friends if you've never mentioned them before? We counted on your good friend Harold and look where that went. I just wonder if you're thinking clearly. If you're depending on people who are dependable. One minute you're in Guasti, the next minute you're in Mount Shasta. What are you going to do if _this_ doesn't work out?"

"I left that pitiful little parish because it was purely a

demotion. If they'd given me something more substantial, I could have gotten on my feet again. But I was going nowhere. If this deal in Shasta falls through, I might go back. But they'd have to offer me a more respectable parish."

"Father Mike, you can't keep bouncing back and forth, just using the Church when it's convenient. Either you want to be a priest or you don't. That was the whole reason you left with me. You hated the hypocrisy. What's happening to you?"

"I'm trying to make a life for us, the only way I know how," he said earnestly.

I looked at his flushed, frustrated face and something inside of me let go. I reached across the table and cupped his chin tenderly in my hands.

"You poor man," I said sadly. "Don't you see? There isn't going to be a life for us."

CHAPTER 30

In February I drove down to Palm Springs to attend my mother's annual Valentine party. This was the big social event she hosted each year at Thunderbird Country Club to honor her friends who had birthdays in February. My brother and his wife was flying in from New Jersey. I knew that Ramona, who shared my Valentine birthday, would be there.

According to Ramona, Palm Springs society had never quite satisfied itself about what really happened. Some peoples' allegiance to Father Mike was so strong that they had trouble believing the rumors. Others discounted the tale because of my mother's drinking. Did Father Mike really take Madge Phillips daughter away or did he not? Did he really leave the priesthood or is that drunk woman just crazy? Unable to reach a conclusion that would satisfy their appetites, many people attended Madge's party hoping for clues. But my family played the game of denial so well, they found none.

On the afternoon of the party I had lunch at Ramona's.

"You hold your head up high tonight, honey. You have nothing to worry about," she said as she stacked the dishes neatly in the rack. "You're beautiful and you're wonderful. There won't be a person at that party who's in a position to judge you."

I knew that two of these guests she was referring to were Georgia Barnette, the office machinery heiress and her husband, Ryan Roberts, an ex-Catholic priest. He had left the priesthood to marry her and she had the money to support him. They had no children and belonged to all the clubs.

Before leaving for Thunderbird that night, my mother had noticed my confidence. I saw her watching me in the dressing room mirror.

"You really have no shame, do you Royal?" She was applying another dusting of face powder to her over-powdered nose while holding her cigarette at arms length to avoid smoke in her eyes.

"No, Mother, I don't," I said, turning to face her. "Not an ounce. I loved that man. And there is something else I want you to know. I had a child. I had his child." These words tumbled out of my mouth with no hesitation. I felt I had nothing to lose or fear from telling the truth. I was tired of pretending.

My mother swiveled around on her dressing table stool. "If you think this will upset me before my party, you're wrong. The detectives have given me their final report," she said calmly. "I already know about the baby."

"How long have you known?"

"I just got the report a few days ago. I haven't shown it to Mr. Hamilton and I won't have my party ruined because of it. Don't you forget that that S.O.B. of a priest has hurt me too."

"How did he hurt you, Mother?"

"That child was my flesh and blood, too." Turning toward her dressing table she deposited a lace handkerchief into her beaded evening bag. "If you want, Royal, I can help you find her," she added softly.

"Thank you, Mother. I've thought of that and I've worried about her welfare. But I've given her up and it's over with Father Mike so I think its best to leave her in peace. All I've thought about is my suicide and how I don't want to live anymore. The pain has been so overwhelming......"

"Do you know where that bastard is?"

"I have no idea."

"Why didn't you come to me and let me help you get an abortion? Why didn't the bastard practice birth control? You wouldn't have had to go through all this heartache."

"I offered to have an abortion in the beginning but Father Mike wouldn't let me. He also wouldn't practice birth control because he was Catholic. He said he was going to marry me."

"That S.O.B. I hope he rots in hell," she mumbled.

"This may be hard for you to believe but I have no regrets, Mother. Do you remember in Hong Kong, when I was so sick and thought I was going to die? How I was crying because I was afraid I'd die without ever having a baby? Well, I'm glad I've had that experience. Giving my baby up is the hardest thing I've ever done, but for me, it is my greatest gift to the world, the greatest gift I could ever give."

"You greatest gift? You've suffered needlessly and caused me to suffer endless pain, all out of your own stupidity."

We heard the impatient sound of a horn below. My brother had brought the car around.

"Whatever you may think of this mess, it is still a disgrace," my mother said, fastening her mink stole around her shoulders and picking up her evening bag.

The private dining room at the Thunderbird Country Club in Rancho Mirage was swathed in red velvet and lace. Heart-shaped topiary trees outlined in tiny white lights stood as glittering centerpieces on each of a dozen tables. A cloud of red heart-shaped balloons clung to the ceiling. My mother went over to the long buffet table to confer with Sanchez, the caterer, who was putting his final touches on his heart-shaped tomato and salmon aspics. The orchestra was warming up. My mother marshaled Mr. Hamilton, my brother and sister-in law and me into a receiving line by the door, in the formal way she preferred to greet her guests.

The distinguished citizens of the desert worked their way through the line. I looked each and every one of them in the eye and shook their hand. If they were hungry for telltale signs of sin, there was nothing in my gaze on which to feed.

When the guests had been greeted, my brother, Merv, ushered me onto the dance floor where all those with February birthdays were honored by the melodic strains of "My Funny Valentine." The cameras of the society page reporters flashed and I held my head high.

JUST BACK FROM HAWAII. Mervyn Phillips Jr. and Franklin Phillips and their wives were honored at a party given by their mother Mrs. Mervyn Phillips, second from left. Central figure is Mrs. Phillips' daughter Royal, who was starting to celebrate a Valentine birthday that night. [Desert Sun Photo]

EPILOGUE

In 1962, in another wave of denial, my mother donated an additional stained glass window to the Indian church and had her marriage to Mr. Hamilton annulled. My brother later told me what my mother had asked him to keep secret: that Mr. Hamilton at the age of eighty-one, was impotent. After the annulment, she had the maids painstakingly pick out the "H" monogram on all of her wedding towels. This was no simple task.

Father Mike continued to vacillate in and out of the priesthood for the next six years. He continued to drink heavily. He was never able to come to terms with the truth of who he really was. In 1967, when he was fifty-three years old, he died at Our Lady of Mt. Carmel Priory, a small cloister in Tucson, Arizona.

I continued to have bouts of acute depression and to feel suicidal. During that time I married a man my age who let me cry and who didn't run away. We had three extraordinary children together. And then I devoted myself to Childbirth Education, teaching parents the preciousness of the new soul. But in a safe harbor I was able to collapse. Finally recognizing the depths of my festering wounds, and with the encouragement of my husband, I sought professional help. My unorthodox Jewish psychiatrist taught me more about Christianity than any Christian I had ever met. It was the beginning of the long journey inward.

LETTERS

To: Royal Phillips
Care of: Chi Omega Sorority House
University of New Mexico
Albuquerque, NM

From: Madge Phillips
310 Patencio Road
Palm Springs, CA 92262

October 19, 1959

Dear Royal: Did you get my donation check I sent to
the sorority house? Please let me know, as I will
have to stop payment if it gets into the wrong hands.
I have wonderful news to report. I have recently met
a Catholic priest by way of the Crockett's cocktail
party. After my generous gift to his parish, he
agreed to personally counsel you. Father Michael
Raymond O'Donohoe has had thirty years counseling
others. I have great hopes that he will be able to
knock some sense into that thick head of yours
concerning THAT good for nothing college boy you
think you love. I pray that our upcoming world trip
will make you forget him.

In the meantime, I want you to pray for my carcinoma.
The doctors inform me that it could be serious. My
new back brace hasn't done any good. I will have to
get a new one for our trip. When I go to Mass this
afternoon, I will do a novena for my healing.

You better be getting good grades, otherwise it's a
waste of my time and energy.

Always,

Mother

May 14, 1993

Connie Mitchell ACSW, CISW
Executive Director
Catholic Social Service Adoption
1825 West Northern
Phoenix, Arizona 85021

Dear Connie Mitchell:

As you requested, enclosed is proof of my
identity. I want to update my September, 1961
adoption file with the CSS. I am not searching
for my daughter but have always kept my file in
current order, in case she wanted information
or wanted to contact me.

Times have certainly changed and I thank
God! Can you imagine all the years of therapy I
have had just to cope with the shame and
humiliation?

Please place the enclosed letter to my
daughter in our file. Thanks for all your help.

Very truly yours,

Royal Phillips

Dear Deirdre Dawn O'Donohoe:

This is the name your father and I picked for
you. Perhaps you will never know it. Every few years
I update my file, just in case you are curious about
your birth mother and father or wanted to find me. I
never wanted to disrupt yours or your adoptive
parents' lives by finding you. The Catholic Social
Services of Phoenix assured me that you were going to
be adopted by a loving, wonderful family. I see by my
correspondence with them that you are the eldest of
three adopted babies.

When I signed those papers in 1961, I felt as if
I was giving the greatest gift to the world-YOU-to
someone. I was! Never for a moment did I not want
you. Never for a split second did I not love you.

Your Irish father was a Catholic priest, 28 years
older than I. He died as a result of alcoholism on
August 9, 1967, at the age of 53.

The forbidden circumstances and closed-minded era
of your birth trapped me in a situation I had no
control over. Please always remember that never for a
moment that I did not want you. I did everything in
my power to keep you. Thank God, todays woman as more
freedom and choices in the realm of adoption. I
married and gave birth to three special cherubs. I
dedicated my life to the spiritual and mental health
and well-being of children. The recovery of my mental
health after the trauma of your adoption has been
long journey.

I hope your adoptive parents have provided a warm
upbringing, spot lighting your individuality. I
already know you are quite beautiful! Every year on
September 16th I say special prayers especially to
you. Feel my love around you at all times. As you
grew in my womb, so also did never ending love grow
in my heart.

Truly yours,
Your birth mother

This is not a work of fiction. Names, characters, places and incidents are real. The material is from actual dated diaries, letters and family photo albums.

The names of some individuals have been changed out of respect and consideration.

ACKNOWLEDGMENTS

Nancy Robinson, my red headed writing pal who offered vast encouragement and coaxed me to enter the Santa Barbara Writers Conference contest. I won first place!

Barb Monaghan, my Illinois "sister" for her Irish knowledge and clever input.

David Cox, the knowledgeable mountain MAC guru.

Anna Worley, my Smoky Mountain daughter of healing and health.

Stella Larson, a deeply concerned mother who possesses much wisdom and creative writing truth.

Randall Pütz, Councilman, my eldest son who has a Journalism Degree. He is always full of guiding and truthful tidbits.

Monte Schulz, Santa Barbara Writers Conference, my writing pal who has always been encouraging and helpful.

Amy Watson Wood, my right hand champion in these mountains featuring support with a young mind in my electronic world!

Sander Pütz, my eldest grandson who is a web design wizard.

ABOUT THE AUTHOR

As an international childbirth instructor and doula for over 35 years, Royal Phillips has taught and lectured in the United States, the Middle East, Central America, Europe, Indonesia and Australia. She has been the teacher of choice for many movie actors and professional athletes. As an advocate for children, Royal has also created and produced childbirth-specific books, audiotapes, and videos. Her documentary, Prince for a Day, chronicles Indonesian circumcision rituals on the youth of Sumbawa and was presented at the Anti-Genital Mutilation Symposium at University of Sydney, Australia.

Royal has been a contributor to the Santa Barbara News Press and a columnist for The Montecito Journal. Her writing has received several awards, including her screenplay Incommunicado, based on her hostage experience in the 1994 Zapatista Rebellion in Chiapas, Mexico. Her recently published book, Ugly Duckling: A True Life Story of Beauty, Manipulation and Murder, is available on www.pamalaphillipsstory.com and amazon.com.

Born on Valentines Day, 1940, in Chicago, Royal is an alumna of The University of New Mexico. She is a mother of three, grandmother of five, and a birth mother of one. She is a world traveler who has visited over 80 countries. Royal currently resides in the Smoky Mountains.

Made in the USA
Columbia, SC
11 December 2017